Wounded Healer

Surviving Childhood Trauma

Lee Lyttle

Manor House

Library and Archives Canada
Cataloguing in Publication

Title: Wounded healer : surviving childhood abuse / Lee Lyttle.

Names: Lyttle, Lee, author.

Identifiers: Canadiana 20210328398 |

ISBN 9781988058702 (softcover) |

ISBN 9781988058719 (hardcover)

Subjects: LCSH: Lyttle, Lee. | LCSH: Adult child sexual abuse victims—Biography. | LCSH: Sexual   abuse victims—Rehabilitation. | LCGFT: Autobiographies.
Classification: LCC HV6570.4.C3 L98 2021 |
DDC 362.76/4092—dc23

Front Cover art: leonartphoto / Shutterstock.
Back Cover art: Amber Konikow (photo of the adult Author contemplating his younger self)

First Edition
Cover Design-layout / Interior- layout: Michael Davie
Edited by Susan Crossman, Crossman Communications
194 pages / 62,300 words.   All rights reserved.
Published 2021   / Copyright 2021
Manor House Publishing Inc.
452 Cottingham Crescent, Ancaster, ON, L9G 3V6
www.manor-house-publishing.com   (905) 648-4797

Funded by the Government of Canada |

To the families and children who have endured and experienced addictions, trauma, and mental illness, specifically to the male survivors of childhood sex abuse. May you find the hope and courage to feel you can live a fulfilling life.

To all the Men who are suffering in silence needing hope. You are loved and needed in this world. And to all trauma survivors suffering in silence. You are also loved.

To the parents or family of children who have experienced childhood trauma, addictions and mental illness. May you find the strength and hope you need.

To all the individuals who feel lost right now and are wandering down a path of uncertainty and fear. May you discover faith and light.

To all First Nations families and children. May you find the peace and strength to walk the road to healing.

Praise for Wounded Healer

"Wounded Healer chronicles author Lee Lyttle's childhood sexual abuse by an older babysitter, how the author learned to cope and come to terms with this experience and how he came to help other victims and advance a greater understanding of the trauma and actions needed to overcome and prevent childhood sexual abuse."

- **Michael B. Davie**, author, *Great Advice*

"Lee's memoir is a testament to the power of vulnerability and candidness in recovery. Lee is embracing their story and giving you a glimpse into the process, which will hopefully empower your own healing. Not only does the book contain poetry in the literal sense, but the entire work is also a work of poetry in action and recovery as an art form."

-**Dr. Jamie Marich,** Founder, The Institute for Creative Mindfulness, Author, ***Trauma and the 12 Steps: An Inclusive Guide to Healing and Recovery***, and many other books on trauma recovery

Acknowledgements

To my dear mother and father, and my step-mother, Janet Lyttle, and to my wonderful aunts and uncles, and my late grandparents: thank you all.

And thank you to all the people who have come along on my life's journey with me, through my recovery and on into the professional world. There are too many to name but I must acknowledge a few: Bill. D and Lori, Bruce and Linda C, Keith T and James W.]And to all the family members and friends who have loved me until I was able to love myself. You all know who you are.

I want to acknowledge with special awareness the James Bay Cree First Nation, and in particular the families and children in the communities of Kashechewan First Nation and Attawapiskat First Nation, who in many ways have given me strength and an understanding of my place in the natural laws of this human walk. You have taught me the great medicine of bringing laughter into hardship. Furthermore, to the many families and children in Kashechewan First Nation and Attawapiskat First Nation: your strength, wisdom, and courage have provided me with a passion to fight further for social justice and you have given me the determination to continue to raise awareness of the devastating impact of the residential schools system in Canada.

And, with great appreciation for Susan Crossman, who I not only view as the editor of this memoir my but also as a mentor who has worked tirelessly and provided me with the motivation and determination to succeed. Also Wendy Woods, and many spiritual mentors whose wisdom has brought me greater insight into self-compassion and love.With special thanks to Michael Davie of Manor House Publishing who was willing to explore my work and I am blessed to receive his insight into the publishing world.

Some events and facts in this memoir are nothing original in many respects—they trace experiences many people have had—but I consider these words to be very sacred as they have come as the result of some very difficult work I have done to heal. They also embrace the many stories of pain and hope

And, lastly, I have a deeper gratitude and obedience to this ever evolving mystery of a higher power which has brought, in many respects, a deeper manifestation of wisdom, strength and guidance to my life. Through people , dreams and nature. That higher power has no doubt been the ultimate captain and teacher for me. It calls me forward, and it calls me up into a higher vision for my life than I ever would have created for myself. I am blessed.

TABLE Of CONTENTS:

Prayer of St Francis

Lord make Me an instrument of Your peace
Where there is hatred let me sow love.
Where there is injury, pardon.
Where there is doubt, faith.
Where there is despair, hope.
Where there is darkness, light.
Where there is sadness, joy.
O Divine master grant that I may
Not so much seek to be consoled as to console
To be understood, as to understand.
To be loved. as to love
For it's in giving that we receive
And it's in pardoning that we are pardoned
And it's in dying that we are born...
To eternal life.
Amen...

- St. Francis of Assisi

I Am My Heart

My justice is my fire

My own sacredness,

And I am the wind that came into that flame.

I am the storm, the fire, the law, the segments of the sky and clouds.

I am the flame that burns into the cliff and clay.

I am the dark parts of the bottom of the river.

I am the light that ripples in the bay.

I am the voice that screams on my own shore.

My eyes and blood and bones are made with dirt and my heart was made from stars.

The twigs that rise up from the ice become my veins

And my thoughts are like the branches that reach out to the moon.

I am my heart that opens and closes.

Long before my heart was formed, I was a silent walker, half ghost.

I shaped the twilight in the shadows

I was reaching the stars for you

Although along a path forbidden in time

I have a heart that's gone mad with Love

Yet, Day stars shine through the forests

In moments

Now I see in carnal eyes, a new angel

Gone astray

Serenity

Because being broken is great, is sweet

And being lost

In my Heart

Is Love.

About the Author

Twenty-four years of professional and personal experience with addictions and mental illness have led Lee Lyttle to the conclusion that we are all imperfect… and that is a-okay.

His memoir, *Wounded Healer* traces his healing journey through childhood trauma, addictions, and mental illness. His hope is to share how creativity and imagination, music, and art, can help people cope in a positive way with trauma of any nature, and he aims to support other male survivors of child sexual abuse, childhood trauma, addictions, or mental illness.

In *Wounded Healer,* Lee shares his raw personal story and truths he's learned about healing from traumatic experiences. It demonstrates how his insights into creativity and the power of the imagination enabled him to take difficult experiences and lean into them, a process, which set him on a path of continually seeking and reaching new edges in life. Lee believes tremendous healing occurs the minute we share our stories honestly with others who have experienced similar difficulties, and that expressing our true identity is the greatest medicine we can ever find.

With 10 years of experience working as a therapist for people who have suffered traumatic brain injury, Lee's insights and training into psychology and behaviour—amplified by his artistic endeavours—have given him the ability to explore trauma healing from a variety of perspectives: experientially and academically, as well as vocationally. Combining insights from western mainstream psychology and Traditional First Nations wisdom and practice through the concept of "Two-Eyed seeing" allow Lee to bring clients to a place of wholeness and wellness.

Lee extends his healing work with various methods of healing he has learned through 12-Step support groups, religion, and various aspects of spirituality.

Lee received a Post Graduate Diploma in Clinical Behavioural Sciences from McMaster University and he is a registered member of the Ontario College of Social Work and Social Service Workers. He is currently a mental health worker serving families on the reserve in Attawapiskat First Nation, Ontario Canada.

Introduction:

Revelations and Insights—The Journey

When I was young I would often take risks in an effort to lose myself, for the emotional pain I felt was great. I was, what we call now a highly sensitive person from birth, I believe.

Many nights I would fall asleep and pray that this would be the last night, this would be the last time of me, and I would hold my breath to play with that feeling. I would hold my breath to the point of almost gasping to see how close I could get to the edge of suicide.

I remember at around age five thinking how smart I was to have the ability so young to think that I could end my life. This perhaps could have been when I began to understand an ego from the inside, an internal machine in full force mixed with false pride and defiance.

I prayed I would never wake up. I would hold my breath as long as I could, and then one day I had a breath that came from outside, a mystery breath. Today I have a voice and a breath that I love, and I want to sleep. I'm comfortable with breathing. I want to be awake.

As you are reading this you may be experiencing some kind of emotional pain in your life, or even mental anguish and confusion. When we begin to see that we are wounded or are broken in some way, we may find that everything we have tried in order to avoid the truth and reality of ourselves has failed, and we are left with only one decision: to either face the reality of who we are as broken beings, and move to accept this, or to self-annihilate.

In some way, you have been led to this memoir and to me, and that means you may be moving into a place of examining what truth means to you.

I invite you to sit and hold and explore these words, words that I've used to try to communicate my experiences. I invite you to reflect on their meaning, and to question yourself about what my experiences might mean for you and your own understanding of who you are and who you are here to be.

I've learned from my own experience, and I will say that pain is okay, *OKAY*, and normal. Part of my pain throughout most of my life was caused by a severe disconnection, a severance, from the world, people, and reality.

At some point in our lives we often start to find that what we are striving to attain is a feeling of connection to people. Nature and reality are really what we are striving to attain. And we ask, "why do I feel this life may be important to me?" I have often had major difficulty in forming and facing this kind of reality.

I have invested a lot of time—time wasted—in running. I grew up in challenging circumstances, that I will explain later. It meant I had to form an alternate reality, a result of the experience of being isolated in my mind and body and soul, and this prevented me from acquiring the skills I needed to face the reality I knew was there, yet which was far too difficult for me to face.

I could not fully grasp the idea that human connections were part of survival; it was a painful idea. Yet connections turned out to be crucial to my development and my wellbeing. That isn't to say they weren't available to me, but because I was so busy focusing on how to survive throughout most of my life, I did not see when and how others loved me, or where they fit in to this process of human connection.

It's frightening to not know who you are. There were many days when I felt disconnected from my life and the world around me, and I really felt lost, as many of us do at some point. At the time I wasn't aware that this disconnection from life had symptoms: they included long periods of restlessness and anxiety that ultimately earned me a diagnosis of Generalized Anxiety Disorder at age 26.

Wounded Healer / Lee Lyttle

Looking back, I am quite positive that I had symptoms of other psychiatric disorders, that I believe my alcohol and substance use masked. I was afraid of not ever having a chance to live a standard, even minimal, life. I became my own medicine man and I decided the basic prescription for my pain was to set out on a suicide mission.

Initially this medicine was somewhat centred in fantasy and deceit, all of which I felt I needed to help me survive pain I considered unbearable.

Fortunately, music and creativity saved me, however on occasion I struggled with my connection to these as well, out of concern that they may have been about obsession and fantasy, and that they prevented me from feeling painful emotions that could ultimately lead me to better my health. I had major difficulties with landing softly on the ground when I was in flight from reality.

Interestingly, but not surprisingly, this was a major challenge in the writing of this book. The idea of landing my story in a physical reality was, and still is, foreign to me. But I now realize I have a choice. Finding my physical life at age 42 is the ticket to the life I had long sought.

It just sucks that I'm 42 already. A therapist once said to me that she didn't think I had an attention problem; rather, I often just picked out random thoughts and ideas from the sky and went through an exhaustive process of trying to discover meaning in them. This in effect was one major reason I felt I needed to write this book: it has been a part of my survival. I needed to finally organize my thoughts (with much help from my editor, of course, with whom I jokingly shared that she may well deserve a PhD in counseling on top of her editing credentials).

I haven't always been a great communicator and this process; on top of the healing work I've done, has taught me to be more transparent and more clear. Forgive me now if you may have to dig a little deeper for understanding: part of me also wants to show you the necessity of digging deep within yourself to come up with your own interpretation of your life and experiences.

Now, at this stage of my life, I am only beginning to understand my thinking and why and how it works. I became so skilled at random thoughts, daydreaming and forming ideas that it became a part of my character, deep inside. The confusing element for me lay in my attempts to understand the difference between creative imagination and a pure need to defend myself against uncomfortable, and painful, thoughts and emotions.

I began to journal and sketch early in my life and many relatives, friends, and teachers empowered me to pursue these activities. They became part of my healing process, yet I often still continued to feel disconnected. Can anybody else relate to that?

When I discovered alcohol, around age 11, I thought my problems with my emotions and thinking were solved, which is a very common, distorted belief among many people who have experienced addictions. Having constantly reviewed my wounded story I realize that we all have a story and now, on the current path of humanity, I believe it is time for us to care about our own stories and what they mean for us, personally, and for all humanity.

I frequently see an outpouring of people's personal stories online, one of the positive aspects of technology. In a way, this unites us. There is one common element we can't deny that we all share: that we are striving to share ideas.

We all seek meaning and connection to others, and to life. People share very personal and vulnerable aspects of their lives with the world. We are more confident now because we are living in the sphere of a common humanity.

The new wave of psychology, sciences, and the brain and the mind, means there are thousands of articles available now containing knowledge on trauma. This points to what appears to be a common drive for humanity to seek understanding of our overall existence and to find meaning in our lives.

In addition, we hear terms such as mindfulness, narcissism, cognitive dysfunction, behavioural therapy, post trauma, and even complex trauma.

Wounded Healer / Lee Lyttle

We hear we are in an age of anxiety, and there are always new perspectives on violence and topics of abuse. There has even been a recent change in terminology, with Domestic Violence now being referred to as Partner Violence, which emphasizes that violence can occur anywhere, in any type of relationship.

I could have easily remained quiet and kept my story to myself. I could've easily left this topic of trauma and addiction alone. More qualified and experienced people have shared their research on such matters already.

Yet, something is happening, I know. Through the current changes in our human and spiritual landscape, I have felt that I, too, can be a part of that stream of consciousness and experience. Hearing my own voice through these words has motivated me. In many respects, although we are investigating more and having new insights into our thoughts, feelings, and behaviours, we may in fact be more challenged than ever to truly experience life in all its dimensions.

As a society we tend to forget it's okay to feel life is scary and it's okay to be frightened. There are many movements and causes and groups out there defining and dividing us.

Although it's important to feel connection and feel there is a cause that merits our support, I feel that in some respects it's important to not get so caught up with that energy that we lose focus on our own personal development.

I was thinking of coining a new term: Obsessive Attachment to Labels and Defining Ourselves Identity Disorder. OALDID. Our understanding of who we are can actually be quite simple. I am both broken and healing.

Examining our own behaviours and motives is critical to spiritual and mental health.

My intention most of all with this book is to trigger something in my readers that will allow you to reach down and discover a path and a story, even if it means understanding the suffering you have experienced along your path.

15

Wounded Healer / Lee Lyttle

It is my hope and intention that readers may identify how they can find what grounds them in life. Ask yourself if there are more possibilities for you in your own journey. What are you searching for, and how might sharing your story help you open up to a sense of common humanity? What might give your story greater purpose?

Perhaps look at moments of suffering in your life, and reflect on how this was managed, or not. Examine what has played a part in your suffering. The fact that we have these stories at all is what makes us fully human. It is a gift to experience despair, grief, and sorrow, for those moments give us the opportunity to *gain* some pleasantness.

By contemplating your own story, you can begin to care more about your experience.

Many of us have experienced loss, tragedy, and disappointment, and equally intense joys, and a sense of belonging with life and others. It is through self–examination that you may see how you have been striving to become more you.

I have always felt unsettled in my life, yet I never used to think of changing my perception—from thinking I was "always unsettled" to thinking I was a person who was simply striving. I always felt I needed to fill some emptiness inside.

Never once did I think this idea of feeling empty was actually where I was most full, where I had the most hidden and mysterious compassion I had never even known existed.

When I decided to write a book, I felt a deep sense of purpose. Initially I was overwhelmed, as I had a lot of flighty ideas and about a thousand journals of material to work from. Poems, sketches, dreams. At times in the process of formalizing this work,

I felt I was losing touch with the reality of how my early childhood trauma had affected me: at times I saw in my own writing where I had been struggling with some truth about this reality. I would go off into another world, living on the edge, becoming my own psychoanalyst in a way.

16

I had to be careful during this process, which I know is common, where I found myself discovering more things that were difficult and that I needed to examine and from which I needed to heal. This was an interesting process, yet also dangerous, to some degree. I remember hearing some good friends say, "Don't go into your own mind alone, because it's like going into a downtown alley at midnight." When I made the decision to write I knew I had to keep in close contact with a therapist, and with close friends and family, and spiritual teachers, as well.

As you read this book my wish is for you to build your own bridge to the message I'm trying to share, which is that there has to be some beauty available to us as we transition back and forth from a comfortable reality we have invented to a state that is perhaps uncomfortable, or bewildering, but which ultimately leads us to greater well-being.

My wish is that you may gain more understanding of early childhood trauma, addictions and human nature from my personal insights and experiences.

I recognize that throughout history, there have been many scientists, spiritual leaders, psychologists, and philosophers who have neatly wrapped up many facts about these very topics. In our current field of study, we are only beginning to embark upon new levels of knowledge about childhood trauma, the brain, and human behaviour. As a disclaimer, I will say I am not in any particular scientific, psychological, or spiritual league that would give me a platform from which to explain such topics.

This is only my personal journey and story. In order to understand my own existence, I needed to find some meaning in my own story, which I believe we all want to experience. One major lesson I have learned during this writing project is that even though I hadn't realized it, I had often already been connected in the past. Although I was "off" many times, there was a physical reality that was constantly changing and grounding me. This was the connection I had and that I craved. However, my connection tended to be with Nature and not so much with people.

Isolation and Judgement

In my younger years of struggle, I told myself that I despised human nature, that human beings did things that were cruel and— for lack of a better word—evil, not in any religious sense, but rather in terms of their destructive behaviour.

My observation drove me further away from efforts to connect. I could only see how people destroyed life. I later learned this stemmed from how hypersensitive I was; my judgments were actually efforts to protect myself from further harm.

My hyper-vigilance and hypersensitivity often became irrational; I read people's motives and emotions very well. When I saw cruelty, I determined that I could find no place in my life for the person performing the cruel act. Yet life frequently requires us to interact with others we don't like. I am sure there were times when other people saw me as someone they had no desire to interact with, either.

I had to learn that it wasn't the human beings themselves that I hated, but rather what they did. I knew this conflict was in me and that was more and more difficult to accept. I didn't realize that all the hard work I invested in developing a better perspective and diligently attempting to connect people to beauty or make a comparison of how life can both hold the beauty of Nature and what I had known as the destructiveness of human behaviours.

How could the natural chemicals and substances like flowers or trees, or the body of water and flowing of Albion Falls in Hamilton, or the distant silence of a cloud, and the quality of the moon and stars have a relationship with the insincerity and fake presentations of most human behaviours?

In this existence I saw cruel aspects of human nature. From people who set out to deliberately cause pain and suffering to others, and even destroy natural life. I began to feel exhausted during what seemed an endlessly lost cause of bringing meaning to these questions. There was a fine line between me continuing to isolate, and grow in acceptance of some truth that apparently beauty and cruelty could co-exist.

Wounded Healer / Lee Lyttle

I had to accept eventually that it was not my career to understand these existential problems. In many ways I brought on my own confusion and in my isolation at times I couldn't see that an early problem of self-centredness was forming.

I simply couldn't see that people who were being the creators of destruction and suffering were actually hurting and suffering themselves, as well, with their own experiences.

I believed in my own isolation that I was the only person who felt this. It also frightened me to think that one day I might, too, be cruel and cause harm, simply because I carry the human experience.

I was able to discover the edge of a meadow and the land and the wind. I was able to see how sharing my connection to this vision could help others to connect with their own nature. Through measurements of their own flame and sorrow, what does this represent to you when you contemplate your own courage?

My hope is that in reading my story, you can discover what connections you have with Nature and humanity. What keeps you connected with life? What in your evolution has helped you to be where you are? What keeps you grounded? Can you see some beauty in any struggles you have experienced in your life?

As you read this, you may ask why you should care about this story. In most of my own personal therapy practices I often see there has been a pattern, also, to my healing. It's been paced out, formed, shaped and orchestrated beyond any power I have been able to muster personally. When I tell people this, they often get confused, and say, "No, Lee, you are the one who is creating your own destiny." I answer that, yes, I agree, I've had some control and I have made some decisions. I've felt the power of choice in my life and I've often felt a sense of independence.

In most cases, though, I often came to realize that the power I thought I had was one whose purpose was to destroy me, and that power is what I call selfishness.

However, I can't deny that there's some mystery to it all.

19

To me, to keep it simple, there is a life force, which knows and appreciates when I am nearing too close to the edge, and it also knows that on my own I might perhaps want to stay on the edge. It's a force that rips me away from remaining isolated for too long. Because my will wants me to stay disconnected. The life force's intention is to keep the bridge maintenance crew working overtime on the structure that connects my mind to my heart.

And what I have discovered in writing this story is that there are times when this bridge has been clearly set up to keep me grounded in my physical world, which I am grateful to be a part of. I remember that when I was a child the most tragic thing happened to me and my voice was taken from me.

People around me often said I was a sweet, shy, and quiet kid. I thought being quiet was a good thing. I didn't want to have a voice because I believed the world wanted me to be quiet. Yet, as I grew up, I really needed a voice. This is where writing came in.

I had a recent breakthrough in my life where I participated in some intense meditation with moments of silence. The beautiful part of my experience lay in realizing I finally felt I had control of my silence and it wasn't some outside force caused me to be silent. In looking back at my past, I saw that the isolation that was not of my own making allowed me to cause destruction in my life.

Edges and Bridges

In my physical life I have always felt drawn to the edge of things and people—I either created distance or held that I was too attached, always sitting right at the edge where the two joined.

I always wanted to be standing at the edge of the street, testing myself against the railway, trying to balance on that unsettled rock in the stream, crawling and climbing underneath the cliffs, jumping from one sumac to the next. I sought out bridges, places where other worlds were colliding, a place in between where something was evolving and forming. I sought the extreme darkness in the forest, or ran after the locations with the most sunshine and light. I've taken the train to the end of the line, and even now live at a gateway to the Arctic.

Previously I lived in a location situated half in a valley and half in the inner city. In hindsight, there may not be any problems with anyone who wants to pursue life at the balancing point; however, I felt initially I was behaving this way because I believed I could not feel security in the "real" world. I had to admit that I truly have a difficult time in finding stability in people, but equally I had to accept that people are fallible, just like me.

Most recently I have learned how this part of my protective personality for the most part had characteristics of dissociation, a very primitive survival mechanism that I formed to defend against feeling overwhelmed.

What a great relief it was to say that! I was always running away in my head and while in trauma recovery I held onto so much with my body.

I was indeed the great pretender and the great observer. Perhaps I will have more insight to share on the impact of trauma on my life in terms of my body and mind as I heal more.

I have struggled for many years with mental health issues, emotional disorders, and addictions. Without getting into labels, these identifications have helped me begin to educate myself on how and what I need to examine who I am. As long as I don't completely form my identity as such.

My examinations are more in the spiritual realm because that is where I can most clearly see the impact of changes in my daily attitudes and actions.

And, in addition, I have suffered through the experience of childhood trauma. I had complex emotions running through me before I had the inner skills to sort them out and resolve them. I had a poor self-concept.

And I knew my mind was fragile at age five, when I should have been developing my imagination, and responding to my new world, and forming healthy attachments, and connecting with others naturally. But this part of my development was crushed inward.

Through many difficult years there has been one element that has served as my foundation: my soul. And my soul remained within me, sheltered by a broken child, adolescent and man. I believe now that we are all hurt and can be broken.

I read somewhere recently, that no one is perfectly adjusted to his or her environment. And emotionally speaking I would add that no one is perfectly adapted and flexible when life stress or trauma happens. This sense of uncertainty each day is perhaps the primary driver of our fears. I would say that the space in between perspective and experience is ultimately the soul.

People did say to me that I could be a healthy person and man, and they were right, because considering the shit I've seen and experienced, I know I'm fortunate.

Why we suffer is a mystery to me, as is the riddle of why some people disappear in life and some seem to power through. This, I've learned, isn't really my purpose to know. I have found we suffer more trying to find out why we suffer. But we do and that is all. No doubt mankind has logged an overwhelming and disturbing amount of human suffering, which reaches as far back as we can recall.

I'm not convinced any of us have gained an understanding as to why we suffer. We just do. My own systems of belief and my understanding of this topic have evolved over the years.

What I felt and explored when I was 16 years old has changed. As a matter of fact, I don't recall that I felt and believed in anything except misery and despair, and the question of how I was going to manage each day to cope with this despair was at the forefront of my concern.

When I look back, one thing is certain: my physical, mental, and spiritual health always improved when I simply sat in Nature and stared at a tree or a bird or some water or a fire. And this is still true today. Sitting under a tree has been a medicine, which has never failed me. As has feeling at one with the sky and clouds, the storms and rain, the dust, shadows, and cold wintery rivers flowing with ice.

Wounded Healer / Lee Lyttle

The way the wind moves and the way the animals burrow and climb, I have always been able to focus on the details of everything, some will label this "hyper-vigilance" but, to me, it is the character of my soul. This underlying force of Nature has also taught me about my own creativity and expression.

During times of heavy despair, when I get out of the way of my own destructive thinking, some natural, mystical event swarms in on me, and completely knocks me off the edge of my despair. I begin to feel I have a choice to make about my mind and where it's going, I have the choice of either digging deep into my despair before motivating myself to change, or wallowing in self-pity and self-loathing and staying stuck there.

A true upheaval of my thoughts and actions is required and, as some of my healing and recovery literature suggests, it seems as though I am rocketed into another dimension when I begin to have an awareness of a shift in my being and thoughts.

While sitting in a meditative state I envision my despair falling from me, like leaves falling from a maple tree in fall at the call of a strong gust of wind. And in that dimension, I'll often do this weird work of self-examination with deep thought and over-thinking—a bloody miracle—and I engage in a complete self-examination of my being, without morbid reflection, holy shit.

Thoughts of a Universe

For a time, I wanted to have nothing to do with the Universe, and I felt disconnected from the world. I developed feelings and emotions and strong beliefs around the notion I was unlovable. And, despite my resistance to the idea, I came to realize my thoughts were deeply centred on existential questions; eventually, I was having thoughts about the Universe again. My wonderment and curiosity about things beyond the realm of this earthly plane completely seized my soul back into the place where it all began.

Many of us reach a point in our journey, I suppose, where everything we've tried stops working and ultimately the Universe is sitting there, waiting.

At some point we all have to encounter our own inner conflicts. And it's often around that time when we also begin to feel a sense of the story we alone have to tell.

All in all, it seems as though I have been catapulted into a quest to understand at a deeper level my relationship to Everything. Today I believe the Universe doesn't judge me, and I have a responsibility to accept it when it comes crashing into my life. In one priceless moment, for example, I can feel the stars blanketing my shoulders, freezing me in place alongside of them. They hold me there; I feel safe. The Universe never moves, and it never speaks, it is vast and endless, tantalizing and knowable. At other times it seems to me as though the Universe can be a gigantic ignorant asshole.

In general, through self-examination, and practicing a healthy approach to my questions and searching, I have been able to find a routine of care—spiritual and otherwise—for myself, and a way to maintain connections with others. My recovery towards a healthy mind and body, and emotional health, can be done simply, through acceptance of my present moment. It may have been one of my greatest challenges to surrender to the coming of love on the horizon and submerge myself in a complete desire to belong to mankind and the human race. To feel like one has found a source of love in our sometimes-cruel world—or even to find love for ourselves in our own cruel perception of ourselves—is, and will always be, a difficult task.

Early Years of Awakening

Spiritual awakenings are not always pleasant experiences and, as a matter of fact, most of the good, positive change I've experienced has been the result of feeling extremely isolated, lost and afraid.

I've come to realize that I think deeply about everything, which is another way to say I have a habit of overthinking things. But this has also brought me feelings of heavy anxiety, which has never felt good to me; when this first started happening I believed I was too young to think deeply. By 2014, I was aware that I felt deep loss, and I experienced frequent moments of despair.

24

Wounded Healer / Lee Lyttle

As I write this, I have a vision of the boy inside me, of all my allies visiting me, and helping me through the pain of having acquired this ability to think so deeply, to the point of paralysis and obsessive sickness of the mind. The vision expands. I see many strangers standing in tall yellow, white, and green grassy fields, which stretch for miles. At a distance I see a young boy with bright white-blonde hair emerging from a field with many adults walking behind him, encouraging him onwards. He is shy and keeps his distance.

I think how different things would be if that little boy I see as me would allow people in, to be close. What person would I be today? I will never know, I suppose. But, as many of us are aware, and as many people say, none of us would be who we are if we didn't experience what we have experienced, regardless of how tough and rough things were. Somehow, I've accepted this as a somewhat positive thought. I began to accept that I was working hard at shaping my mind to overcome dark clouds and impending destruction, not just because I was willing, but because there is a part of me that wants to survive beyond my own cognition.

Memories and Tears

A trigger or memory recall occurs when a sight, smell, taste, touch, or sound brings forth to my consciousness a deep memory of experiences that were either traumatic and unpleasant, or positive.

Throughout my life memory recalls—almost all of them traumatic—have no doubt had a profound impact on my emotions and my psyche. But through recovery and many hours of therapy I have taught myself to view triggers and memory recalls as simply tools, which can help me examine my environment and myself.

I no longer have to feel dominated by negative and devastating past experiences. I've come to realize that the brain is really an amazing organ that wants to heal and protect us.

In my youth, memories of the sexual abuse I had experienced as a child would trigger days of crying in my bedroom, and I would occasionally look out the window into the dark night. My muscles tensed, I would feel intense pressure in my chest, and my throat would fill up with emotion. I did not realize my body was responding physically to the trauma I had experienced. Crying and fear were a release; I was scared, and this was my way of shutting down and closing up.

My crying episodes were frequent, and I recall wondering at that early age, "Who or What is hearing this cry, where is this pain directed?" I remember thinking, even at the age of six or seven, that this amount of crying was not normal and I was afraid I would never stop.

The window screen became the filter through which I screened my perception of life. Below, I could see the large parking area and the tops of the neighbouring townhomes. The lights of night comforted me and I stared and stared until I fell asleep. In addition to this, I recalled how my fascination with other lights, for example the glow worm toy and Lite Brite set became regular self-soothing tools for me to help me become calm. There is a reason and purpose for those stimulants for children. However for me I absorbed every single pleasant sense around me I could. I was already surviving and didn't have a name for it.

The presence of the wind, every detailed crackle of it, made its way through all the moments in my space. It created an intense calm that often broke through my pain, and the pain I was already feeling was loss, yet I could not find its name.

One night in particular, at around age four, I again found solace at my window after crying for several hours. I believe something opened me up to an idea of power and Nature, and I realized there was a difference between human beings and this other Power. Something dug deep into me.

It was around dusk, and I heard some voices and chatter outside. I looked down and studied the people running in and out of their homes and cars, some holding their coats over their heads in fright.

Straight out my window I could see a large formation of bats flying in sequence, circling the parking lot. This had an impact on me. My stomach at once grew calm and I also stopped crying. Witnessing people in a vulnerable and frightened state actually helped me cope. I saw that human beings could be vulnerable and broken, as I was, although their issues were different from mine. I had already started disconnecting from people because I had seen humans as cruel. They took things from others.

I had formed a perception that humans had the potential to threaten me, and I had become highly tuned to reading behaviour. I knew when people were being selfish or behaving badly. I saw that when people were full of fear: it caused them to do things, which hurt other people, perhaps because they themselves wanted to survive, and be safe. It was a complex thought for a young boy to have.

I witnessed how the natural world, with the swarming of the bats, had a force I felt went beyond the immorality and sickness of human behaviours, and it was a force that actually made people run. Little did I know that this theme would become the ultimate foundation for my life. Even to this day I love to see the power of Nature—such as in a rain- or snowstorm—change people's behaviour. As Kurt Cobain wrote: "Weather changes moods." (Kurt Cobain, from the song *In Bloom*, 1991, from the Nirvana album *Nevermind*)

Insight and Healing

One day early on in the course of my trauma recovery I was driving down the highway. Traffic was slow, but I had been having a reasonably positive day and I didn't feel really stressed about anything in my life. I felt good and healthy and confident.

All of a sudden, I felt a panic come over me and I started to zero in on all the tires on all the vehicles around me. I was looking at the black rubber tires and watching them spin.

Then I realized something had triggered me to think of when I had been at the home of the man, a babysitter, who had sexually abused me. I was two years old, and the father of my abuser had been making model cars with me.

27

The model car kits have small rubber tires that you glue onto the frame of the toy car. Almost immediately I acknowledged the sensations and memory I was experiencing, and I thought, "it's crazy how my brain works," and I had a chuckle.

Within 10 minutes or so of acknowledging my trigger, I was back on my merry way and the panic left me. That moment I had to respect my brain for what it was doing, and I had to acknowledge I was powerless over it. This was one of the first major experiences I had with trauma where I had an insight, which actually helped me. It allowed me to use this experience to start thinking of triggers as learning opportunities rather than overwhelming experiences I needed to avoid and escape.

I am grateful I was able see with clarity the connections between my environment, my memory, my emotions and my thoughts. This to me was a sign of health. I would soon learn that triggers were my greatest companion as they would be the tool I would need to open myself up to deeper healing work.

Connecting in Nature

Over the years, my days have become increasingly marked by the bright fire in my belly, which I now see as an indication of resilience and skill, and my nights have become filled with whispers of calm.

Even so, I have travelled down many other paths into extreme despair, loneliness, fear and self–destruction. Yet I've always returned to that night sky and those bats, Nature's night creatures.

I found I could re-create many aspects of the power of Nature through my imagination but also through the physical world around me, placing my hands in the ground and dirt, touching a branch or weed, catching mice in the farm fields, and lifting rocks secured on the bed of the creeks and streams to search for salamanders. It was as if this discovery was my way of uncovering something new in me.

These experiences in Nature are where I learned I had some control and when I explored, nothing stopped me, and nothing judged me. The environment just seemed to sit and watch me playing. Sometimes I shifted leaves and grass around to examine the light of the sun and create my own shadows. My time in Nature was, and continues to be, limitless.

This may have been my way of striving to gain a sense of belonging in the world, but it was also a result of my anxiety over not being able to connect with people. In many ways it was also a way of escape.

I thought many times over the years that it would be nice if there were no people in my physical world because I felt that people made the world ugly, yet I could trace this feeling back directly and simply, as I will explain, to my experience of trauma. Through it all, Nature was my beacon. This narrative explores how that has played out in my life, and I've seasoned it all with talk of dreams and my own interpretation of spirituality.

In addition to the harshness of my experience with addictions, recovery, and despair, I knew I was forming a deep sensational experience between my flesh and life itself. I have been thrilled to bear witness to kind or gentle experiences: a person opening the door for someone else, the small strands of hay falling off the back of a truck, and much more, all of which, for me, have played out in a reel of slow motion activity. A lark flying and swooping towards the Earth, the sound of crows in the fall, and the smell of the moss on the limestone rocks in Red Hill Valley in spring—these were the ties which bound me to both physical reality and a sense of wonder.

I loved watching the clay streams through the Red Hill Valley and the bottom of the creeks and waterways of Stoney Creek and Mount Albion Falls.

I remember going back to those environments and observing the changing grooves of grey and red that constantly molded and shifted into colors of brown and dark brown, as the water wove in and out of rocks and moss, and pebbles, and smashed along the creekbanks. The waterfalls and creeks were a natural magnifying glass beside which I sat and contemplated change and it was all wonderful.

From about age eight on to today I've had a total love and respect for Southern Ontario: the Bruce Trail, Redhill Valley, Dundas Valley, Valens Conservation Park, Niagara Escarpment, Lake Ontario. I'll always owe a great debt to these landscapes and others which functioned as a major part of my therapy journey.

When not in Nature, I struggled, but I also knew I could not go too far into the natural world because I still knew I needed people. But it was and is fundamental to my notion of being truly alive and connected.

My early experiences of interacting with the natural world helped me develop a sense of being. It remained for me to see how people could also bring fire to my life. That possibility was there, but it took some work for me to find it.

The first time I cried in the woods I really began to see my soul and my vulnerability, and I found my first real sense of communication with the trees.

The cycles of Nature unveiled a purity of interaction and this lay, also, in the way the trees communicated with the sun and the water. It all showed me the profound power of expression and response. Nature created a space for me to be safe.

When I cried, the trees stared at me and simply listened. I felt secure, I wasn't judged. It was unfortunate at the time that I could not fully grasp the reality and importance of developing the human connections, which were going to be crucial to my well-being. That isn't to say it was unavailable to me. There were many opportunities for this to develop but I was so fucking lost I couldn't tap into it. This is what hurts.

Earlier in my life I knew I would have difficulty; in a way I accepted I might never achieve this crucial ability to interact, and I remember saying to myself, "Fuck it."

1 Despair and Sorrow

The severity and sweetness of the winter landscapes and storms that day held me captive. Little did I know the snowy and icy terrain would turn out to be my protection and guardian in the days to come.

It was sometime around 1980, and I was living in Edmonton, Alberta, with my mother and father in a small townhouse. For the most part, I seem to remember that during this time we lived a somewhat quiet life, with the exception of house parties my parents hosted. There was a lot of drinking and drugs, sometimes some fighting. I am seeing more and more how my adult life has been affected by my childhood. It was a classic case of, for lack of a better term, "dysfunction."

As I grew up, I realized that in some way I had to develop an adult's perspective on my parents and my environment to help me learn how to accept and forgive them. And I think that hard work is paying off because I believe I am truly not held back by past negative experiences, but rather have seen my parents and their lives as being full of personal battlegrounds, which in most cases they just couldn't escape.

It was not my responsibility to help them, and I wasn't the cause of their problems. It was interesting to learn, however how children can learn unhealthy coping skills by watching adults who also have had to develop unhealthy coping skills. I have taught through years in recovery myself that one major common characteristic of childhood trauma is that the child often blames themselves for any wrong thing that happens.

When I witnessed family conflict as a child I remember making comments such as "I wish I was never born," and I thought that I was the cause of the violence, or the centre of it.

31

I ask now, why is it common that children blame themselves for how adults behave?

It wasn't until I was an adult and had the gift of working in the child welfare system that I started to see how I myself had been neglected, most of all emotionally. This was the truth I had to examine for my own sanity and peace.

Being able to understand the positive aspects of triggers has been helpful. On the one hand I have been able to see the difficulties some parents have, yet at the same time I still understand that parenting comes with major responsibilities.

A whole chapter can be written on my specific childhood and the issue of healthy family development, and maybe that will unfold in other material. But the seedy path leading to the moments of my ultimate, shattering trauma was not just the result of being part of a family in distress. I can't blame my parents for the sickening act committed against me as a child.

I do believe my Mother had done everything in her power to protect me and watch over me, in general, but she made the decision on one particular day for a neighbour to take care of me.

What occurred as a result has not changed how I feel about my mother. I love her just the same. I also forgive my Mother for the part she played in the unfolding of my trauma,, although, in order for me to heal in some way, along the road to my recovery I had to express my anger and confusion, and be honest about emotions the experience unleashed.

I know people in my life who have been less accepting of parents, but I know that despising her would be dangerous territory for me to explore, as I see many adults who don't live life fully because of past experiences and resentments. They become stranded in the act of blaming other people for their unhappiness.

I knew I had to accept early on as well that my father had his own needs and as difficult it was, I let it go that he had left, for whichever reason I do not know, and, in many ways, it doesn't bother me. It happened.

Wounded Healer / Lee Lyttle

In the Neighbour's Care

I don't recall the particular date and time I ended up in what was meant to be a neighbour's care, but I was probably two years old.

I can recall the ice storm attacking my window and I looked out, a few houses down; I saw the gates of the Hell house that was occupied by that other family. I recall an uneasiness, an unsettling anxiety in my tiny gut, the indication that something was not right. I sensed an evil power was present.

The house appeared to be covered in red soot and the smell of model glue and paint permeated the air. The driveway held a series of car parts dripping with grease. The path leading to the house was maintained, perhaps to cover the destruction, which permeated the spaces inside the house. The man stood at the door, an overweight shadow hanging from the front porch light. I was to be protected through the night. My Mother was in my hand.

My life as I knew it was about to be lost, enslaved to many years of pain and despair and fear and confusion. I recall my hand passing from my mother's care and into the hands of the stranger.

She couldn't have known. I didn't know at the time why she had to leave me there, what decisions she had made, what emergencies had occurred. For all I know, my mother did trust the elder man of this home to protect me; it happened to be his son who caused the abuse.

I remember entering the home. The smell of body odor consumed me, and dirty clothing littered the floor. I knew, even as a child, that this was not right.

Something inside told me that my childhood would slip through me, my guts were sinking, and I couldn't lift up my arms, I couldn't even scream, as I felt I had lost my voice. My mother kisses me. The door closes. The older man sits at the kitchen table with a toy model box and he shows me how he was putting the model together. I was excited to see the toy and excited to be building something.

Wounded Healer / Lee Lyttle

I can't recall how time passed but I remember being taken downstairs by another, younger male. I notice the quality of the airdrops, and it is thick. On a shelf lay the grooming props, Star Wars Figures and Toys. And the ground is filled with dirty clothing. I am stuck. The ground reaches up to take hold of my legs. Darkness falls upon the room. I know as a child I need to escape, but why should I run? I am with my guardian.

I remember the smell of dampness, maybe mold. Clothing and bed sheets were scattered. Something inside me was signaling a threat; yet I didn't have the proper language and physical strength to do anything, even remove myself.

I recall growing more aware of losing control, of becoming increasingly unable to recognize myself as he consumed my innocence. It was then that the breath of a dark ghost awakened within me. I sank deeper into the despair laid out for me by the enemy, the man who had taken my power. I gulped and asked for help, but I was suffocating. Something within me broke. I wished with all my might to somehow slip through the fence rail and escape to the other end of the yard. Away from the predator, away from me.

In the distance, beyond the line of approaching squalls, this idea of an enemy began to grow like a dark shadow within me, another aspect of my being that was building prison walls within my mind and soul. Seeing the enemy was like an experience of going to a war which should never have occurred. It left an imprint on my psyche, like a foreign agent, or a disease that hijacked my thoughts and emotions, a gorilla in the cage in my mind, or squirrels in the attic, but no pest control number for me to contact. It was the enemy in the form of a committee, with another strong voice of self–criticism and an evolution of self-hatred.

I saw the road that met the yard. That was where home was. A place that wasn't as safe as Hell, but was significantly less punishing, or so I imagined. In one moment, I could sense my flesh and the object that I was to the enemy, the man with whom I was to form a bitter lifelong connection. This enemy knew nothing of my sacred soul, it seemed.

Wounded Healer / Lee Lyttle

I knew then and there that I was now a part of a struggle, an inner battle and I was going to fight a war with no plan, no strategy and no weapons. There was no declaration of hostilities, I was allowed no preparation for this war, there had been no history of conflict. I felt I had been injected with a disease and that disease was disconnection and unwarranted fear. Something far beyond what a five-year-old boy should ever have to experience.

Looking back, I see now that in some small way, I was remembering, not experiencing, my pain at the time, and I thought I had already survived the traumatic experience, I had already accepted it. Yet I didn't recognize who I was.

The future of my life was to be something I knew even then I could survive. In the same reflection, I sensed it would be fucking difficult, for sure. How cruel the world was, opening right up in front of me, and already I was cultivating a sense of danger and fear, even though I sensed that deep inside I could accomplish much in life, more intense was the sense that I was deeply and severely damaged, far beyond what I could comprehend.

Over time I learned creative ways to dissociate and avoid the pain generated by the recurring thought that I was dead conflicting with the fact that I was alive. Every day, at every hour, I saw my hearse and casket waiting for me. But I would never step inside because I knew I was alive and in many ways saw some beauty in life. I was the only one who knew of my early death, this death that was premature and endless.

As I am laid down my voice grows silent. My throat is paralyzed. As I look up to the ceiling, I see the red, powdery soot falling down over my body. The hand reaches for my clothing and a cold chill permeates my belly. A hand touches me and forces his mouth over my genitals the hand also made me touch his genitals.

My body lay there, crippled and cold. The man is in his sickness. He is not a form of human. His face is deformed and misshapen. Like the devil himself, he breathes the stench of waste. Waste and disease pour out his every orifice. A mind does not exist. Flames are consuming me; black flames, darkly unnatural.

Heat surrounds every move of the snake and villain who holds me captive. The world I had been beginning to know is crashing outside like a black mirror. And the little world inside of me that I was just beginning to grasp becomes crushed in a single act. I hadn't even known my thoughts, or experienced my emotional self, and the inside of me hadn't even let anyone truly in before this monster crushed every fibre of my being.

My fear of people and my distrust begin. Rage fills me, yet I cannot express it. Pure rage suffocates me. I feel my heart beating rapidly, and I feel as though a billion tons of concrete are crushing my chest. My shoulders grow heavy; I am now a ghost to this world, at a time when life is fragile.

I am weak. I can feel my eyes sinking and my stomach is nauseous. *What protects me? Where did my life go?* My small five-year-old body grows empty. I cannot regain my self. It is as if my guts have been torn right out of me. My thoughts and emotions are paralyzed. I heard it said somewhere once that children who have been traumatized in this way are assaulted by the memories it generates, as well as by the initial act of abuse itself. Their feelings of anxiety and fear are compounded by the battery of sensory airstrikes that are levied against them every waking minute.

Again and again, I questioned what my senses were telling me and I wasn't sure if the feelings I had gave me a green light to accept them as being real to me, or whether they represented another inner assault that I had created because I thought being sensible was a disease. I can't think of how many times I have had to defend my thoughts and emotions against the unsolicited attacks of my own mind. All because of one single act of betrayal that probably took less than 10 minutes to commit.

I've spoken many times with my mother about this time in my life, and opened up about the emotional devastation it caused me. I've had to gain courage and forgiveness, and the call to peace of mind required that I not get caught up in the sickness of blame and resentment. I know my family members blame themselves and are trapped in the horror of feeling responsible for what happened to me. Yet this didn't change what happened. It happened.

I have had to be careful to keep from falling into the trap of putting other people's feelings ahead of my own. I have matured now. I own my own past in many respects, without taking ownership of that crime. While writing this memoir I opened a difficult conversation with my mother, and it ultimately became part of my healing process.

My mother said she had needed to go to work and could not find a babysitter. I know in her heart she wouldn't have consciously neglected me, and it became apparent during our conversation that she blamed herself for what had happened to me. I tried to reassure her that I held no resentment towards her, but this conversation helped me to tap into a sense of anger, perhaps not directed at my mother, but simply at the trauma. And our conversation helped me to find a way to express my anger in a healthy way, one which brought us both a little more peace, and a stronger bond born of sadness shared. And this is why I focus my energy on my helping career. This is why I value my work on behalf of social justice.

Sexual trauma is an epidemic evil in our world, and it is tearing families apart. It devastates the people who have been abused and it negates their potential. It shatters their hearts and gives rise to addictive behaviour that has enormously negative social impacts. If I can in some small way take the benefits of the healing I have painstakingly achieved in my own life, and put it into the service of others, then I will feel my own traumatic experience has been, not a burden to shame and negate me, but a powerful engine for personal liberation, for me and the others I am privileged to assist. Perhaps there may be a little underlying anger remaining within me which may benefit from further examination, but I trust that if there is, I will have the strength to manage it.

Aftermath

After the Event, I saw that inside me was born an idea of darkness, and it permeated my now-lifeless body, animated it and gave everyone, including me, the illusion I was alive. I sank into a long unfeeling rest, from which I was unlikely ever to awaken. I was never to smell, touch, taste, or see the skies of the world outside, cocooned, as I was, into my perceptions and thoughts. I crawled deep inside myself and remained there for many years. Nothing could rock me out of the disconnectedness I felt. No symbol, no act of human love, nothing, or so I believed for many years. I've known death before life itself. I've known injustice before justice itself. I've known darkness before light. I've known victimization before freedom. I've known despair before peace and awakening.

One night, days or months after the trauma, I found a small plastic bag when I went to bed and I tore it up into a small piece of plastic, which I tied so tightly around my penis that it hurt. My mother took me to the clinic and the physician had to delicately cut the bag off.

I wonder what the adults were thinking? What was the professional doctor thinking? To me, looking back now, this was clearly odd, yet I am not sure if anybody questioned this behaviour. This for certain was some kind of psychological response to the trauma that had occurred, yet there was no answer or solution to the real anguish I felt inside. This may have been a cry for help. Children are amazing that way, to express emotional discomfort by any means they feel they can. After working in Child-Welfare, I would perhaps now see this as something to inquire more about. Yet maybe the adults just never paid attention to what reasoning I had. We may never know. Yet now, we would definitely see this as a red flag. I think, man, that was brilliant of me, because obviously I did not have the words to explain what I was feeling. I now recognize I was acting out of trauma. I would be years on the path, which led me from despair to hope.

Somewhere around that time I discovered that my mother's nail polish had an effect on me that felt good, only because it numbed me and I recall what a genius I felt I was to have the power to change my feelings. This likely represented my first addictive relationship with a substance. Nail polish held me until I could develop more sophisticated methods to numb myself. When I sensed I could not cope or manage my responses to life and reality, I then turned to anything within my reach that brought me out of my discontent and fear.

The Birth of the Other

The trauma I had experienced was to be supplemented over the years by many instances of bullying, adding to my impression that people were sick and cruel, and this I associated with death.

Perhaps the loss of hope and death I felt was associated with having an awareness that due to this form of abuse I was unable to build a true identity because again I was being shaped by the strong environmental and psychological impact of bullying.

Around age six my family moved from Edmonton to Calgary and I transitioned to a new school. One day at school a bully confronted me. An older kid and his buddy had trapped me on an outside staircase located at the side of the school, and he chose me as the object of his vengeance.

With every shove he gave me I felt the harshness of the fact that there was no apparent reason for the beginning of the bullying, and there seemed no end to it, either. My whole world became shot through with it. A pattern of cruel circumstances had already begun invading my life and that made it challenging to see positivity in the world and in people. It added to an unconscious and anxious desire to avoid life and people and places.

My days would start off bright and hopeful, and then the unbearable walk to Ramsey Elementary School would unfold. I felt the towering bricks of the school on the hill looming ahead of me. I could hear the other children talking, but their voices came to me faintly.

I would spend most of my time daydreaming, examining my death or obsessing over the numbness I was feeling. At times I would also scour the halls watching for the humiliation my peers wanted to heap upon me, not caring anymore if they caught me and spat on me. During one bullying incident an individual somehow got me to open my mouth while the other spit right inside it. I ended up vomiting afterward. Each day I grew more dread-full of the school and its strangers.

Whereas in my younger years my imagination had saved my life, allowing me a safe place to escape, it now created confusion within me, blossoming into an instrument that created doom.

I was starting to see how frightened of my own mind I was becoming. I did not have the language or ability to make sense of things. I did not see there was a difference between distorted thinking and clear thinking.

There were moments of darkness, and, equally, moments of reason, understanding and wisdom, and they fought for dominion over the lush ground of me. War. At times I felt so powerless over my own mind that I shrank from the sense of duality inside me. There was the damaged self inside, and the self I wanted the outer world to see.

The knowledge I was starting to develop about myself was intense. I heard somewhere that a child's development, or anyone's, for that matter, is disrupted when living arrangements, cities and even schools change frequently. And children who move many times have difficulty building and maintaining connections.

This was true for me and I began to see how my own circumstances allowed me to avoid any connection with life and people. I remember promising myself to never meet anybody because I knew the friendship would never last. This certainly prevented crucial developmental growth.

I recall my fascination with details when I was a child, and it started with books. I was captivated by maps and diagrams, pictures of planets and space aircraft, and illustrations of buildings in space, even maps of the events at the OK Corral from the Wild West era in America.

I loved anything to do with construction, representations of life, new ideas, weather patterns, how tornados are formed, and storms.

In science class I remember making the solar system with craft materials and Styrofoam. I loved models and robotics and lights. Books with pictures were my angels.

Somehow, I was starting to equally become resource-full in my own way by visually exploring my external world.

The allure of maps was particularly powerful. I think this may have been because I needed to see how things were laid out; that still holds true today. I needed to have directions and a plan for where I wanted to travel. And still today I like to have a plan for my travels, both on the outer landscape of the planet and around the inner landscape of me.

As a child, I continued to find and develop my safety in Nature, especially down in the forest area around the Bow River in Calgary, Alberta. It became my refuge, my place of safety, and my place to connect, and it helped me escape the growing inner turmoil with which I had to contend.

Walking home after the storm, he looked at his feet, and the new pair of winter boots the principal at the Ramsey School had given him. The school was a common-looking elementary school built in the heart of the east end of the city. In the front part of the school facing the street stood a large tower with a clock, and an entrance. Behind the building there were three long hills that smothered the river. At times the young soul would wander off and venture along the river after school.

Flights of Death

The belief that I owned the feeling of death within my own soul was the only thing that gave me a sense of control. In some distorted way I believed the sickness I felt within me made me mature, however it was completely maladaptive.

I also always hung around people who were older than me, partly because in some way my pain gave me thoughts and a language, which helped me relate better to them. There were many problems with this, of course, one of which was that it impaired the natural process of my development.

Misery came to claim me one tormented thought at a time and often distorted my self-concept. I came to believe I would never be alive again to the real, natural person I might have been. This belief grew so painful I had to either really work to abolish it or fight to keep it separate from my life story.

Eventually, a major shift happened in me and I chose to slowly and painfully dismantle every old belief and idea I had about who and what I was.

I consciously began to redefine who I Am. Who was I, besides a person who had become a ghost of himself, dead? I was the only being I could see who was both wearing skin and was filled with bone, yet whose belly was full of nothing but pain. I learned to cope. The overall trauma wasn't what was killing me, but the feeling that a living death raging inside of me was. Even at age five I'd sensed the sorrow of death. At age eight, and 12, also.

*****

I attempted to make sense of the world through creative expression, a pursuit, which enabled me to quiet the thoughts and uncertainty of life. I often felt the world was trying to keep a secret from me. In those moments, I felt fragile and futile, no sense of existence, just flesh, blood and bones, and broken memories.

Deep-seated sorrow wove in and out of the fabric of my being. In isolation I would struggle with my madness, generating a pure inability to communicate any real, normal, human emotion. I worked hard at developing a space to hold these dimensions of me.

Nature became my treasure chest, holding them, holding him, holding me. Trees and clouds let me become enmeshed in the details of the environment around me. I merged with clouds reflected in a pond or the clear bottom of a marsh, tadpoles swimming out from under a lily pad, or a garter snake making its way along the edge of the valley hills.

When the wind made its way through leaves, rearranging them, I could relate to those loose twigs and dust as if they were parts of me. I felt a growing active participation in the wilderness outside of me that was a reflection of the wilderness I was walking in within my soul. Throughout my youth I also sketched and painted various images and interpretations of my dreams. I found solace in art and I continue to paint and sketch today, especially landscapes and other pictures of Nature I had taken.

A majority of my work was surreal. It kept me grounded. It was my way of cultivating those bridges I was building to safety. On my own.

What was it that the world dreaded, what secrets was she holding? What is inside us that constantly cries out to explain our story? The river near the school had provided me some sense of security—a structure for life that could crush any enemy that came his way. I knew and was aware that my young soul had developed an imaginative life to survive and it worked but it also had limits I later learned prevented me from building connections with others. This was my tool to drown out the anxious apartness I had felt towards reality. I had started to form a new structure inside me where I could seek refuge. A new Him. I started to form new escape patterns to free myself of uncertainty. What a beautiful concept to have. When the storm is right there, Nature will provide shelter. This will save me, I thought. He thought.

In my mind, I was also forming a method of survival, although it was not a normal one. Gaining a living concept of death prepared my mind to become numb, and shut everything down when others came too close. Although unhealthy, in the end, I finally had the power to escape. Many people I have met who experience addictions often say that the addiction, although destructive and serious, had in some ways prevented them from complete annihilation. Prevented them from further harm and destruction. And, although it was abnormal, it was survival. I know the other thoughts that started to occur often were of suicide. This was the ultimate harm and form of destroying myself. This began to plague my thoughts from time to time.

Down at the River

One day, before coming home from school, I journeyed once again down to the river. Fascinated by the current that was endlessly flowing in and out of the frozen ice along its banks, I decided to reach down and touch the frigid waters.

As I reached further, I sensed the cold numbing texture of the water. And, like any normal person, I rapidly shook my hand out of the river. Looking up at the sky He noticed the winter clouds drifting through the sky. The white glowing sphere of the sun was blinding him as it seeped through the partial cloud cover.

As if this would be the last chance for me to be there at the riverside, I reached into the waters again and enjoyed the moment of feeling. Then, in a sudden breath, I felt an object beneath the surface. I pulled it up and recognized it to be a bird's feather, perfectly dry. He then placed the feather delicately in my schoolbook.

At home I had several books in my room. In every book, you would find some items that I had found along the paths I had walked. An artist you could make a perfect collage from them. Some scrap metals from the railway yard. Branches, broken glass. Torn photographs of strangers and, of course, a wide variety of feathers ranging from magpies to pigeons and jays. Nothing made sense except the changes of Nature, the endurance of life there taught the young soul life itself. Nature had educated me daily. I taught myself to foster how I wondered. This was His greatest form of resilience, too.

As in every animal or plant, some hidden natural process was at work in me. The roots never see the sun and the sun never has a relationship with the roots, yet they both depend upon each other. They speak to each other underground. As in the natural world, I felt a relationship was being formed underground within me. The natural word captured the cycles within me and made sense. I could see darkness and light through trees and the sky. And these were the only real senses I could understand.

Wounded Healer / Lee Lyttle

The darkness of winter came near to an end. The changing of the season was at hand. A new life prevailed. I could not see the cycles within me—they were broken in some way—but I could witness the change in the seasons. The late winter winds caused the snow to drift and when I witnessed this, I could feel things shift in me, too.

On a trip to the mountains in spring, the young soul was opened to a new wilderness. As the family drove along a dirt road by a lake, I gazed in wonder out of the window.

With my window half-way down, the fresh mountain breeze swooped out of the lake and blew through my hair: I would observe the Universe out the backseat window, never growing fearful of anything I couldn't explain.

As we drove along, I noticed the cliffs bending closer to the sides of the road. Some rocks hanging in mid-air far above the massive foundations of the land below it were indescribably wonderful.

A short distance later, the car stopped abruptly. I wondered what was wrong. I fought to slip back into a mode where I could create judgment, but there were no senses to be found. The man driving pulled the car into reverse and stopped alongside a small cliff. As I looked up, an image against the slope caught my eyes.

There on the edge stood a timber wolf. Its back was hunched, and shining fur made him appear like a statue overlooking the Earth. I again saw every detail of that moment, that mountainside. And the wind moved my hair with promises of a sweeter tomorrow.

I was amazed at this glimpse of life and it created in me a feeling of safety and retreat. I wished to inspect the creature further, but the car drove off. And thus the wind started seeping through the window.

When I look back now, I see the proverbial "young boy on a highway in the mountains who is guided by a wolf."

I believed my life turned into a light I could live in and whenever I could use my imagination to think of these peaceful signposts, these visions, I could have a new survival kit. I started to feel I had a chance to break free from living with the terror of someone else's despair.

I knew this was a tool for me to somehow escape from the intensity and complexity of my emotions. Earth was my cure for grief. I could examine any new difficult emotions I encountered appropriately and I was starting to learn skills to mentally reorganize my thoughts and see more and more how patterns really dominated me in my thoughts and behaviours.

Many people would call this resilience. I do not use this word lightly. Yet when encountering difficult emotions and thoughts resilience is not always 100% effective. From ages eight to 18 there were many times where I was in flight from sadness and death and even some true joy. My hope came from knowing that, through it all, I was still moving forward in my life as best I could with what I had.

2   Music as a Pathway to Healing

My mother used to say to me, "if you could remember your math equations like you remembered lyrics from Pink Floyd and The Beatles you would have had a PhD in physics by age 20."

Other themes have emerged and remained my foundation throughout my life: my imagination and my music. I cannot completely explain how much power and influence music and the many aspects of this art have had an impact on me.

Of course, we can all identify that music in itself has only enhanced our human experience. For Survivors, it can be a lifeline. In truth, my exposure to and relationship with these two pivotal aspects of my world would take years to explain. One thing I know for sure is that when I first heard Pink Floyd's *Dark Side of the Moon* album on cassette, I was hooked.

Then one year my mother bought me the Bryan Adams albums, *Reckless* and *Cuts Like a Knife*. I also had a powerful reaction to music when my Uncle Rodney drove his Ford Truck around at my grandmother's place blaring "My Sharona" by the Knack through his stereo system.

And there was the time my Uncle Gerry Lyttle and Aunt Sonya played David Bowie for me on an old reel-to-reel system.

My first vinyl was Jeff Beck's *Blow by Blow*, followed by Rush's *Permanent Waves*. Other powerful music that influenced me and continues to resonate with me is Christopher Cross's " Sailing," Bryan Ferry's "More Than This," and Howard Jones's "No one is to Blame."

These songs remind me of my summer family trips from Hamilton to Calgary, Alberta and the Rocky Mountains, as well as British Colombia.

I also loved bands like Steely Dan, Gerry Rafferty (Baker Street) and Neil Young. Of course, on another entirely significant realm were the early country and 1950's music, which my mother and father introduced to me.

Today, I have a doubly nostalgic experience where I am recalling 1950's music I discovered in the 1970's, and that I still listen to in 2020. Sometimes I feel this sense that I am not from this time, but rather I was born in the 40's or 50's.

Music and Managing

Over time I've realized that the interaction of sound and my ears represents healing for me. Music was a drug and as I grew up I believe it helped me cope and keep me grounded. I grew so attached to sounds and rhythm and lyrics and the creativity of music that I lost all chance of acquiring the ability to form normal attachments to people.

I felt that a short five-second melody on the piano or by a string ensemble, or in a Richie Hawtin Techno sequence, provided me with more parenting than I had received in years. The transitions and loops from Aphex Twins's *Analogue Bubble Bath* and approximately three years of cassette recordings from the Dr Trance radio hour on 102.1 FM provided emotional nourishment and became the warming hand that gently stroked my head and back when I felt I was in need of comfort.

Percussion and guitar often helped me to sit and reflect on the transitions in my life. And I was incapable of capacitating the infinite amount of love and support that has been available to me throughout my entire existence.

The friends I did have growing up introduced me to new bands as well. Mr. Kennedy had a preference for REM, Mr. Henderson had a fondness for Tom Waits and experimental bands like Mr. Bungle (a spin-off of Faith No More). Mr. Henderson also re-introduced me to female folk artist Melanie, which undoubtedly pushed me through certain insecure times through high school.

Wounded Healer / Lee Lyttle

Little did I know as well, until my Aunt Ellen once told me she used to sing "Alexander the Beetle" by Melanie to me when I was a babe.

Other friends introduced me to bands like The Doors, Tool, Screaming Trees and Smashing Pumpkins, Aphex Twins, Morrissey, The Smiths and The Housemartins. Many times I remember Mr. Kydd bringing me a coffee in the morning and playing the new album of Aphex Twins, *Polygon Windows*.

There was a period, too, where I was introduced to what I believe was one major band: The Cure. The dark moody and melodic vocals of Robert Smith, mixed with very unique guitar playing and drumming and synths, sort of reminded me of a pop version of Pink Floydesque material.

In that era, as well, I was listening to Depeche Mode, in particular the song "Somebody." I remember how quickly I remembered the lyrics to that track. New Order also led me into a pop rock interest that shaped my teen summers. And I worshipped the New Order's *Substance* album. I would watch music videos instead of cartoons, and I started to include classical music in my interests, and even jazz.

Claude Debussy literally struck a neuro system that brought me a sense of peace and physically calmed me, yet also allowed me to daydream and exercise my imagination.

Later I stumbled across Philip Glass and more contemporary artists like Gavin Bryers and even Jonny Greenwood from Radiohead. Then of course there was my what I call my "disco years" attending the many Raves in Toronto in the early 90's, which led me into interests in electronic music, most importantly trance, ambient and Jungle or drum and bass.

In fact when I look at those experiences I was equally drawn and attracted to the subculture where I saw creativity and art through individual expressions and dance.

On one occasion, I think around 1994/95, I actually found myself dancing on Electric Circus in Toronto. "E," as it was referred to, was a long-standing live dance show with weekly live musical performances mostly showcasing dance and electronic music. I'm still trying to locate that old footage from Much Music. I believe the live band when I was on the show was Tony Toni Tone, with their hit "It Feels Good."

Sometimes I think if I had another career it would actually be dancing because It feels so good. The music nurtures me so much that I could easily dance in one minute to John Cougar Mellencamp wailing, "Hurt so Good" and then jump into a mosh pit with Ministry playing, and then sit in an orchestra and let the piano and strings put me in a trance or dance into some pop or classic rock.

It's quite fascinating as I look back at the influence of musical patterns in my life. It was probably around the same time I was exploring the new music and instrumental, experimental sounds from CBC brave new waves, that I stumbled across Tubular Bells by Mike Oldfield, which led me into listening to more early Rush albums like *Caress of Steel, 2112,* and *Preludes of the Future.* In that same realm I also loved the Queen track, "Prophet's Song." I was drawn to this theme of fantasy within the lyrics and in many ways they inspired me to draw and paint.

One major song always stood out from the rest. "Child in Time" from Deep Purple. For some reason I really fell into the deep dark moody sounds of that song. I think the percussions really made that possible for me.

As for many people, music became a language that helped me understand many things.

Music and a desire for creativity can either give us sanity or help us self-destruct. As a child, this is what began to define me, and shape my character and personality.

However, I was unable to learn to cope with my inside character, which was developing as a "hurt person," and I began to believe that my hurt self was my only self. This part was forming and shaping into a victim, full of self-pity and fear. I began to form many personalities that allowed me to manipulate circumstances and cope with my feelings of self-pity and resentment.

50

I was struggling to determine what pain constituted "appropriate" emotional pain. I was seeking comfort in the thought of pain, and ultimately it led to further self-destructive behaviour. Emotional pain and victimization were my gods, and functioned as my primary defense against the reality I was experiencing.

Along the way I discovered lights could soothe my senses as well. I recognized that my increasing reliance on alcohol was self-destructive and that I had to survive by seeking out other ways of soothing and "medicating" myself. When I was a kid I used to bring a flashlight to bed and manipulate the beam on the ceiling.

Messing with the light and the dark shadows gave me a sense of control. I would bring lights under the covers with me and it felt like I was building a universe of my own where I could live.

More External Stability

Books, movies and television were also critical to my stability growing up. They've been crucial to my healing and development and have helped me in many ways to reflect upon aspects of human emotion and spirit. Through this cultivation of external remedies, my only task was to not escape too far from my internal dilemma, yet learn to blend the external with the internal world.

In particular, I loved the film adaptation of Toni Morrison's book *Beloved*, starring Oprah Winfrey. In many ways the imagery and the difficult topic the story exposes, resonated deeply with me. I could relate to the emotional toll, which comes from living a life full of pain and trauma, while immersed in all the complexities which affect the human soul. The movie had a tragic storyline with a supernatural twist and I recall reading that Oprah had fallen into a depression after completing the movie, which didn't surprise me, given the nature of the film.

Although I knew that the arts were a powerful force for me, I still struggled with a deep need to connect with others. When the time came for my recovery life, however, I did have to acknowledge in some aspects that I had to be cautious of the elements of my connection to the arts as sometimes they may also have an addictive component to them.

For example, I remember talking to a therapist once about my experiences of heavily listening to hours and hours of Radiohead tracks, or even wallowing in the mournful old tunes of Merle Haggard and Willie Nelson. In some aspects this was where I could rationalize and justify my own depressive state and it could be dangerous if left unchecked. It seemed to bring me into an emotional state where I had a false sense of control over how I felt. Yet again, if not managed well, this could send me into a few hours—or even days—of self-pity. Take in particular the albums like Radiohead's *Kid A* and tracks on other albums like *King of Limbs* and the tracks, "Codex" and "Scatterbrain," from the album *Hail to the Thieves*.

Throughout my teen years, music was still my saving grace and despite the drinking I discovered two very crucial bands which paved my way into a new adventure in sounds and musical tastes: Red House Painters, in particular the album *Ocean Beach* and Low (*Secret Name* and *The Curtain Hits the Cast* were particular favorites).

I also found my way to early techno and house music, and the rave scene in Toronto. By the time my Grandmother Lyttle passed away in 1996, I was listening heavily to Talking Heads, in particular their album *Fear of Music*, and the song "Heaven."

Film and movie soundtracks like *Stand By Me, Footloose* and *Dirty Dancing* began to influence my development. I became reliably submerged in music. I was always and still am very impacted by sound and music. Music has been the feel good, go-to mechanism which saved me many times. I was always able to find great relief and peace in it. And to this day I believe our Higher Power communicates with us through the language of music.

There is no doubt that music was and is today a powerful grounding tool for me regarding healing and dealing with my past trauma. However, I had to learn to be very careful and limit myself at times as its power brought me into places where I would be in too much of a trance with my emotions. One way I am learning now is to write and create my own music, which I love.

Wounded Healer / Lee Lyttle

Wrestling with Myself

In the late 80's, I joined the minor Olympic-style wrestling team at my elementary school, and when the city championships were held I was the leading athlete in my weight class. I sat on the bleachers awaiting my event filled with anxiety; my distorted emotions and thoughts were my only company.

As I looked out onto the floor at the matches currently underway, I turned on my yellow waterproof Sony Walkman and began to play a cassette a friend had lent me. I pushed the play button and on came *Across the Universe* by The Beatles. My soul knew I had to fight with fire and what better way to sort out complex emotions, than participating in the exercise of listening to music, especially The Beatles.

The cassette tape itself was made of clear plastic and someone had written "The Beatles" in liquid paper on it. There were a variety of other tracks from *Let it Be* and the *White Album* on the cassette, as well.

The difficulty with having complex emotions—such as shame and despair—was that I obsessed over the lyrics in the song, especially where John Lennon sings, "Nothing's Going Change My World." This hit me to the core. It was almost as if I accepted I was going to stay hurt for the whole of my existence, and this frightened me. Although I couldn't interpret the song, those lyrics had an immense impact on me. I took in the tone and the melody. The song empowered my belief, although it was false, that nothing would *ever* change me. I recall saying to myself that nothing would ever change me, meaning I wanted to be a victim and remain a hurt person my whole life.

I was destined to live in only my world of hurt. My complex emotions began to turn into complex thoughts, which often caused disturbance for me. *Across the Universe* played through and I rewound it and listened to it over and over, and I squeezed out a few tears as well, until it was finally my turn to hit the mat.

I was nervous entering the gymnasium floor, and I felt the adrenaline pour through me. I was competing, I was ready. My stance sharpened and I entered the circle and faced my opponent. We immediately dropped to the floor and I had him in my strategic move, the crowd cheering me. But then he pulled through and my strength to keep him pinned waned. I held on and tried to gain some balance, however within seconds he had my shoulder and legs and I was done.

Later in the day, I learned I had been awarded third place in the city for my age and weight. I did feel a sense of achievement and even pride, yet it was short-lived and quickly became overshadowed by my sense of not deserving the honour. I was hard on myself because I didn't do better, and I also fell into despair because I was experiencing social anxiety and low confidence in myself. The positivity started to happen when I could see where I was really making a conscious effort to lay aside painful emotions. And more therapy on my own, such as reading and meditation helped me sort this out, as well.

Patterns and Confidence

As time went on, the pattern repeated itself. In retrospect, although I had racked up some good achievements, I didn't have the emotional skills to really acknowledge them and allow them to build my confidence. I felt deep inside that I didn't deserve to win anything. To this day it has taken much practice for me to fully gain a sense of achievement.

It was an emotionally-confusing situation: I wanted to achieve, but once the achievement had been won, I hated myself because I couldn't absorb it into my personality and character.

I judged myself, even though people were patting me on the back. I wasn't receptive and couldn't sit alone with my emotions. I started to develop an inner critic who was a complete jackass. I often spent time sitting in a black space of emptiness, which today I call self-pity. Today I know that self-pity, if left untreated, can turn into depression and further isolation.

Moving On

In 1984/85, when I was about eight years old, my mother and my new stepfather moved from Calgary, Alberta, to Ontario. I recall hearing that when people, or families, move frequently, the upheaval is difficult for everybody; it's hard to meet new friends and let go of current connections.

This time spent travelling across Canada gave me a chance to be with my mother closely, and I could sense her anxiety about everything. I was angry but I also found myself starting to develop a sense of responsibility for her choices and fears.

My mother never married my father and I knew she had her own deeply-seeded difficulties with her own life and upbringing. Yet, she is a very courageous woman and she learned how to survive, much like I did.

Growing up in our culture, and particularly, in many ways, in my own family, I felt I had to hide this sensitive side out of fear of being ridiculed and, of course, others may see this as a weakness. This is very common.

I often felt that some males—especially older males— were threatening to me as a result of the trauma. And at some point in my life, I began to suspect that if there were any true/real deity or Supreme Being, it would be one which took the form of creative intelligence and this gave me permission to embrace the idea that there is a divine feminine aspect to my being.

Even though the cross-Canada move felt to me like a sudden severance of my youth, I did acquire a sense of adventure.

I knew that even though we had moved for circumstances most likely beyond my control, it was an opportunity. And this, I believe, is when I found a sense of adventure in travelling long distance by roads or highways.

Looking back now it hurts me to see and think of how hurt I felt and how damaged I believed I was.

Now I can only hold and comfort that young boy who I see in my mind's eye.

In many ways, through displacement, I was receiving some answers to questions I was already asking myself.

As defective as it was, again I grew an independent sense of survival to work things out on my own, which was also problematic because I never learned how to seek out and take on the support that was offered to me. I believed in some way that life just wasn't for me.

Something interesting about death, however, a river that never really dies, gave me a sense of a life with room for eternity. And, oh! To enter into some painless state for eternity would be my goal.

I would often wonder where this river would flow. I admired the natural force of life. It was calm on top and I heard once that there were rough currents underneath, much like my newly-discovered sense of my emotional self.

Many experiences had taught me not to trust any type of process I encountered, and fear of others led the way.

I could be a calm person on the outside yet terrified on the inside. I was running from the physical world as fast as I could, not realizing how far I was actually running.

Socializing was a challenge for me and I had a severe inability to bond intimately with people.

I did have some role modeling from many uncles and aunts and cousins, yet I continued to struggle with social skills and morals as well as maladaptive behaviours that on some occasions also harmed others without me knowing how my behaviours were affecting them.

Wounded Healer / Lee Lyttle

Summers

My mother and father had made arrangements for me to visit with my father and his family each summer for a good five or six years after we moved to Ontario. I always felt the need to rebuild and nurture relationships within my family. Although I was able to form some healthy bonds and attachments, I always felt a deep detachment at the same time and I knew in many ways I was seen as the typical back sheep. I loved travelling back to Alberta during the summers, however, and I was proud I had grown up there.

I remembered the park and slides in Westwood Park, a local city park and community hall in Edmonton Alberta. It was close to where my Grandmother Lyttle lived and my family visited it often in the summer.

Meeting with my other cousins brought joy and temporary relief from the pain of detachment or my awareness of how difficult it was for me to detach. However, I can only recall being aware of people my age during those interactions. I had an inability to form an emotional connection.

Whirlwinds of thoughts and images grew. Just past the park there were two small hills and then a baseball diamond. After we played and jumped in the sand we would march to the variety store like paratroopers in WWII. We would drink bottles of the soda Tahiti Treat and eat Old Dutch potato chips. I would climb up and jump from the sides of the old silver metal twirling slides with my cousins, Jeff and Jeremy.

It was during this time in my life where I could see my thoughts becoming more abstract, particularly around the fascination I had with death.

One day while visiting my Grandmother at around age eight or nine, I became curious about the books around the coffee table when I found, there in the wooden cupboards on the side of the solid wood frame, some other books. Someone had ordered a series of quality-made hard cover books created by Time Life.

Three of the books contained detailed information, stories, illustrations and pictures depicting the western era in the United States of America. When I flipped through the pages my eyes would always be glued to the images of the dead outlaws hanging, and other death-related pictures. I was forming a morbid curiosity about, and fascination with, the images.

There were pages of photographs of the outlaws, clothed in black and wearing black hoods, alongside the white-hooded bounty hunters of the Midwest. In one shot the hoods were cut so the eyes could peer through. And you could tell the sheriffs had stuffed the hoods rather poorly over their own heads. I was fascinated by the illustrations of the maps and homes and the history of the OK Corral shoot-out.

I wondered how the dead souls of the outlaws could peer through their black hoods, how could they see, is it just darkness now, emptiness? I saw some small crack in their eyes, death seeping through, but they were looking at something, I thought. This public display of death intrigued me. In some form the dead man could feel the pain and numbness of the hanged.

In other photos I studied the cold pale faces of the dead and wondered how the sunken eyes and bruised features had gotten there. In some ways I can see that these images were another description of the inner bruising of my own pain. I was desperately becoming more aware of the importance for me to identify with something that could make some sense to me.

From that day on I couldn't push those images out of my mind. Every time a visit to Grandmother's was near I would get anxious about going to see the photos. I began to think as though that was my identity; sadly I can identify with maybe being motionless, yet looking alive.

I wanted to be still, I wanted to wear that mask, and I did and it did cost me. The most severe consequence was that it helped me spend years growing detached from the world and its people until I could honestly start to examine what this fascination was trying to teach me.

Moving Out and More on Moving On

By 1994 I was 18 and felt it was time for me to move out on my own. It was as though I was being driven to grow up fast, although I did trust this new change. I was reliable and employable and had had various jobs along the way, and this was my saving grace. I moved into an apartment on Melrose Avenue in Hamilton, Ontario

The ability to be a hard worker helped with structure and gave me a sense of responsibility, which I loved. However, within a year my alcohol consumption had increased dramatically.

At 19 I was consuming hard liquor, and large amounts of it, until I would get sick and black out, ultimately to the point of wanting to never wake up. I knew and accepted that I was on a path of self-destruction and it was just a matter of time. The idea was comfortable to me. I thought that if I drank enough I could shut down my body and stop breathing. I had begun drinking alcohol around age 13 and my drinking patterns had been increasing in intensity ever since.

Little did I know at the time that I was in the midst of a fatal progression of an illness, mainly spiritual in nature. During high school I learned new ways to hide my pain from others, and alcohol and the party life were part of the recipe. On the outside I seemed to be doing well academically and I was successful in many ways. I joined my high school's football team, playing a defensive position as a corner back, a highlight throughout high school, as I loved the physical exercises and competitiveness. Even though I may have been distracted by my inner turmoil, I also did surprisingly well with getting decent grades.

Mr. W. and I

As a kid I was proud that I took risks to try and connect with others, even though I couldn't form healthy attachments and I had a hard time seeing what was unhealthy for me in my connections. My mother tried her best to connect me with various activities and she enrolled me in Atom Football, full contact. I loved it, especially the competitiveness.

Like many others I found sports to be an effective way to manage my energy and my underlying aggression because there were rules you had to follow. This provided some structure in my life. Perhaps I will share more of my love for athletics and sports in a future memoir.

The Universe will set things up for you knowing you will need to be structured in something, which will allow for expression and learning.

However, I knew my personality development and overall social development was lagging. So I tried to make social connections, but I always had a sense of not fully belonging or participating in each moment, so I did what I thought I was supposed to do; I acted and pretended. It was a typical hallmark of having low self-esteem.

I allowed my social circle to heavily influence me and create my identity. I withdrew inside and my defenses became more elaborate: sometimes I would lie and steal. My anxiety was growing more intense: I felt I needed to keep others from seeing I was hurting.

I attempted to develop and foster new relationships with others but my own deep raging fears, centred on my fear of abandonment, still crippled me.

Why should I put effort into really connecting, I wondered, when I believed my relationships wouldn't last? The belief may have been false, but overall I felt everyone was really seeking something; what would I have to offer?

At age 10 I joined the Hamilton Minor Football Association. One connection I attempted to form there was with young Mr. W. I first met him when I was eight, soon after my mother, stepfather and I had moved to Ontario from Alberta. He lived in my neighbourhood, only two streets over and close to the ravine by Greenhill and Quigley Road, in the east end of Hamilton.

Mr. W was a running back on my team, and he was quite the player. He was also a Chicago Bears fan and he introduced me to the music of reggae singer Bob Marley. Hanging out with him was glorious—I looked forward to it.

We attended the Festival of Friends outdoor music celebration together every summer for about five years and almost every Saturday we'd catch the 57 Nash bus to King Street and Queenston Road, then head west to downtown's Jackson Square.

We walked endlessly through the markets, watching people and counting our change to purchase a Cinnabon. We grew close. Hamilton was interesting in the mid-to-late 80s. Rock'N'Tees was a great store to visit, and the first musical t-shirts I bought honoured the Ska band, The Specials (to whose music Mr. W had introduced me), and the Violent Femmes.

We also caught a glimpse of the Forgotten Rebels playing live in Hamilton. Mr. W introduced me to English Beat and other Ska bands, such as Madness; from there I recall picking up on the early sounds of The Police. I particularly liked their album *Regatta De Blanc* and the track "Bring on the Night."

I was so proud and felt so grounded with this new connection with Mr. W that I took tentative steps towards building trust with those around me. I suppose I felt a sense of authenticity with our connection, in how we interacted and talked. I started to feel I was developing normal skills for life. It seemed my friendships were thriving. I still had some moments where I was anxious because I still felt separated from others. Simultaneously I was attempting to learn new mature ways to survive.

But when a socially difficult situation occurred that I felt I didn't have the skills to navigate, I would deliberately do things to smash myself down and, as they say, sabotage very good things.

Looking back now I can see indictors I was attempting to form healthy connections by allowing myself to show some vulnerability, by sharing about my life.

Friendships were still a struggle, but Mr. W. represented a positive start in a good direction and in many ways he challenged me by getting out and exploring new social situations.

I remember Mr. W raved about how he had been hired as an extra in a Trident Gum commercial and he started going to Toronto a lot.

He was the first of my friends to get his driver's license and he bought a 1990 Honda Prelude. He and I started to frequent the early Toronto rave scene from about 1993-96. He was going places, I thought! And I admired that. But he grew more quiet over the years.

After High School

Meanwhile, as I became accustomed to living on my own, and drinking more, my inner fears and insecurities began to take hold in earnest.

I began experimenting with drugs. This progressed quite quickly for me.

became obsessed with hiding my pain while trying to continue to cope with complex trauma-related emotions.

The effort was exhausting and made me feel more isolated. I began to manipulate people, including members of the opposite sex. I know now that this was my attempt to fill another empty void I saw in me,

I wanted to be wanted and needed and loved, but I was selfish. I didn't really know what healthy attachments were.

In later years, being more honest in my life and in therapy was tough work. I had to examine my wrongs and clear the wreckage I'd left in my past. What helped me was the ability to see that my past is a great asset, as I am able to share what I've learned along my road in a way that helps others who have suffered similar experiences.

This is where the tough work of self-forgiveness and taking responsible action lies. This is why I am going through the tough work to share my experiences and my voice; this is my motivation to make living amends and develop my professional life as a social service worker, teacher, and counselor.

I've learned the value of not blaming my past for causing me to act out or behave poorly and I've become fully accountable for my actions. This has brought me a feeling of integrity and, even more importantly, humility. No one really intends to hurt other people.

At the time, before recovery, I did not pay attention to the needs and wants and desires and goals of others around me: I was too focused on my own shit and I was selfish, falling apart on the inside.

I lived in a temple of victimization and learned helplessness, and I was obsessed with placing myself in situations where I could be abandoned or rejected. The strange contradiction and dilemma, of course, was that I also feared rejection and abandonment; yet in many ways I was choosing social situations where this would happen. False, temporary relief came through drinking massive amounts of whiskey. He was always prompted to run and hide.

I remember Mr. W coming to my house one time soon after I had moved out on my own. I was isolating myself from the world. He told me I needed to get outside. I sensed he was caring and I suppose until this point no one had ever really known me that well. He was looking out for my well-being. His desire to care for me was another normal aspect of intimacy that was foreign to me, yet I took it at face value; I was still immature.

Around that time, Mr. W also left home and began living on his own in various places in Hamilton and Toronto. He appeared to be moving around often and I was curious about this new independence he had.

When I visited him, his apartments usually had little-to-no-furniture, and little food.

Mr. W also began to talk differently and almost became obsessed with his own isolation. His tone of voice changed and his outlook on reality became uncomfortable for me to see. It's frightening when you see your friends suffering and becoming more isolated.

He did say to me one time that he felt he might have taken some bad drugs at a Rave. And then I put the two together; perhaps this was a form of drug-induced psychosis. He was drifting away. I began to grieve the loss of my first real friendship. His descent into drug addiction was similar to me losing a sense of reality myself. We were both sinking but as time went on I began to take steps towards a life of sobriety.

He called me from time to time, as he had held on to my phone number.

Then one day when he dropped in on me, he barely made eye contact, which I put down to the fact that he knew I was on a path to health but he was not there yet. This caused me to feel what I've heard people refer to as "survivor guilt." I offered him some tea but he refused it. He talked quickly and appeared obsessed with his own thoughts. I wasn't sure if he was high or simply delusional. I felt powerless to reach him, and I felt he could easily lose his grip on life.

I hadn't seen him for two years or so by this point. He kept repeating how happy he was for me that I was sober. There he sat at my kitchen table, and I was flooded with feelings of sadness, and memories of the joy we had experienced in our youth. I was feeling anxiety and compassion and fear for his well-being. We talked. Football, Music Festivals.

One day he dropped by my place without telling me he was going to visit. He didn't say much to me, yet he began to cry. There, under his dark black hoodie, his eyes shuddering and filled with tears, he cried unlike anyone I've ever seen. It was like there was a sign of hope breaking through, along with a silent veil of fear and confusion about his current state. I knew Mr. W was suffering. It was like he was crying for me to take him out of the darkness he was in, but all I could do was provide a shoulder.

Wounded Healer / Lee Lyttle

Mr. W held my hand and then pulled me closer to him. He cried as he hugged me, and then quickly got up and left. After that I did not see or hear from him for three or four years. I heard once that he was living on the street and I prayed for his safety. It seemed as though all the interactions I was having with people occurred around the time when they themselves were falling apart. I can see how I was falling apart, too, yet I was gaining support.

Then, one day as I was walking downtown I saw an individual walking towards me with his head down. As we walked closer I recognized that it was him and I called his name: He walked right passed me and as he walked, he looked into my eyes… but he was gone. He did not say anything. His mind was not there. I fell into a shocked state of disbelief and I cried. He continued to walk and I knew he was lost. I couldn't contain myself. I don't know if he knew who I was, or where he was.

All the years we had spent together in our youth seemed like a false life, but I knew he was sick. I knew in many ways he had blown up his brain with substances, and combined with past mental health issues, it had become too late for him.

From 1999-2010, he called me every now and then, almost as if he wanted to check in. I often offered support and redirected him to seek outside help. But the disease of addiction was devastating. He started living in and out of shelters, although he had tried once to live at home.

Whenever he called I would ask if he wanted to go for a coffee but he always declined.

I never gave up, though, and one day he surprised me and said, "sure." I met him downtown. We sat for a bit. He was still nervous and looked around a lot but he listened to me.

He looked disheveled and his behaviour frightened me a little: it was clear his mind was gone and this had an impact on me as he was the first person who had been close to me who had fried themselves. It was a profound and tragic change.

65

He shared with me stories about our past with our rave parties, and growing up, yet the conversations were disorganized. And he would start talking about religion. This was a beginning.

In many ways I identified with him, and I could relate to his fall into isolation, and his desire to return to health. He shared with me that he was living in a lodging home for those who are homeless with psychiatric needs. I was happy he wasn't on the street.

My heart is somewhat full in the certain knowledge, now, that Mr. W. is receiving the support he needs from his family and friends. It is a tough journey.

Through the years I saw some of my other friends really fall apart from the abusive things they were doing to themselves. I know how my friends were raised and how each of them coped with their own struggles with mental health, their environment, and their family. Mr. W. was no exception to the rule. For years I would often wear a Chicago Bears NFL cap in honour of him.

3 Dimension of My Spiritual Self

At one point in my life during the years of 1995 and 1996 I started to grow more aware that there was a real conflict within me. As I mentioned previously I still battled with a constant separation or disconnection with a part of me and another ghost I was seeking.

I knew deep inside I could no longer run and hide from the unresolved trauma in my life and the creep of mental illness.

I must have found some grounding pattern in simple dialogue with others; little did I know, I was also starting to develop my co-dependent traits, such as only listening for where people were hurt and how I could help them.

My co-dependency became the foundation for how most of my communicating with others developed.

One major trait of these patterns was the fact I had poor boundaries between myself and others. I basically had none. Later on, I realized this wasn't the healthiest way to start relationships with others. Through these relations I am not proud that I engaged in promiscuous behaviour, and I hurt many people.

My fears of intimacy meant that once I started to see others I was close with challenging me around my own faults, I realized this was not how I wanted the relationship to unfold, and I ran to avoided this deeper level of closeness.

The truth was there. I knew I had to not just rationalize or blame my decisions on my addiction, but I had to be honest and search deep into how immoral I was. I had to take responsibility and honestly work toward changing.

There is currently much debate in our world about addictions and behaviour, as some people tend to blame their behaviours on addiction, but this is only part of the problem: there is also an avoidance of taking ownership and an avoidance of being fully honest at work here. I do get stuck in this area though. I think it's more complicated, for each individual is different. People called me out on my behaviour and I had to become responsible. The crisis of the break-up of a high school relationship with a girl led me into the circle of 12-Step support groups. I knew for some real reason this crisis had a deep impact on me and I wanted to finally look at the deeper issues I had.

I saw that my pain was deep, as were the consequences of my behaviour. I thought more of suicide, running in front of a bus, hanging myself, running in front of a train, self-inflicted knife wounds, and, furthermore, a self-inflicted gunshot. My thoughts of killing myself became an increasing concern. I hated myself. I was done hiding and running. I stood up and I surrendered.

The Adventure within the Crisis

I mustered up a new willingness to look at my crisis as a new adventure and this perspective helped me, even though my life was at a critical stage. New bottoms were being presented and I had decisions to make: to flee or face what I discovered.

At some point I realized I needed to get close to others without the fear of being abandoned. I also needed to identify that although my health required me to engage in self-reflection, it was also hindered me from actually developing intimacy skills.

I started to see that it was in my daily interactions with people that I actually started to get grounded. My intellectualizing and self-discovery and experiences with finding ways to self-reflect would not protect me anymore.

I began to see how trapped I was in my own self-absorption. I was a victim of my mind and emotions in many respects. I wished to be anchored in my own pattern of recovery, yet when presented with difficulty I resorted back to the Self.

One very important factor that arose out of writing this memoir was when I had a breakthrough regarding my style of thinking. The creative process of writing this memoir helped me look at my own stream of consciousness, and once I started to see limitations with my self-reflection, I was then able to move into more skills to keep grounded in real life. What a gift this was for me! To actually see for the first time that my trauma self and trauma thinking had a chance to survive and thrive much like everyone else.

There is no doubt that through my early recovery part of my willingness to learn about myself was prompted by my dedication to reading and studying books which explored such topics as spirituality, philosophy, religion, behavioural sciences, and art.

Taking time to read was a practice of very powerful grounding for me. One of the first books I read was *The Road Less Travelled* by Scott Peck, along with the *Big Book of Alcoholics Anonymous* and the *12 and 12*. Others included *The Sermon on the Mount* by Emmet Fox and numerous journals, daily meditation books. I read *The Bible, Living Buddha Living Christ,* by Thich Nhat Hanh, and *The Language of Letting Go,* by Melody Beattie, a pioneer in the area of co-dependency.

Furthermore, as I developed a more disciplined understanding of spiritual practice, and as I maintained my limits with understanding self-reflection versus morbid reflection or avoidance, other materials aided my new paths of self-discovery. For example, *Staring at the Sun*, by Irvin D. Yalom, helped me overcome later phobias with death and then, of course, *Self-Compassion Mindfulness,* by Kristen Neff.

I also found a fascination in small pocket books with references to spiritual or religious material, prayers, and tools for contemplation.

I continue to refer back to these materials to progress in my spiritual growth. My educational seeking towards them is always evolving and new perspectives are always formed. So, indeed, I found reading time and interactions with people started to become tools that helped my get out of my traumatic brain.

I learned early on that teaching ourselves about what we experience or what and why we are thinking the way we do, helps us to cope with it. If you are suicidal and sad, read about it. Now we have amazing technology, which allows us to access education on subjects like never before.

Early in my recovery, I noticed the importance of little connections, like seeing the bus driver, the store clerks, the banker, and the friendly, familiar faces of people at coffee shops.

During my time living in Dundas, I frequented Taylor's Tea Room for a nice cup of vanilla Earl Grey and a scone; as a matter of fact, when I first began this memoir I found the Tea Room a special place to get focused and start going through my notes. I loved the cream butter as I placed it over the jam on the scone.

I also found pleasure in the smiles and laughter of the rooms of AA. The host of friendships in my brothers and sisters that I was to become involved with could not be explained. For the first time I was in a fellowship and I felt I belonged. There are thousands of names and people who have entered into my path; it would take another chapter to include these experiences.

James W., Kurtie Boy, Keith T., Frank and Joy, all my beautiful friends at the Harmony group of AA and the Early Bird of AA. I've met what feels like a million friends in this journey. The practice I gained with making an honest effort to listen to others, allowed me to feel my first real form of connection.

And I actually loved listening to others. This is how I started to see that people were all hurting and lost in some form, and yet I started to realize I am not responsible for their experiences.

I remember hearing a man once sharing that it is natural for one to automatically jump up and hand someone a tissue when we see they are upset. Yet, he went on to say, we may actually interfere with an important healing experience for that person. Listening and being silent were the greatest lessons for me.

The connection with listening to others helped me to see how I also had the capacity for positive emotional connection with others, and it enabled me to have real physical connection with people.

Maturity

I used to think was I a phony, because I have empathy for people when I "should" still have a deep hatred for humanity because of what happened to me. Ultimately, though, I realized I wasn't abandoning my own cause, I was maturing. Now, I show my love for others by listening to them, and actually in my career my greatest tool for work is actively listening to others.

I often feel this is how I am contributing to the world, how I am giving back to humanity.

The more richness I found in simple conversations and listening, the more I wanted. It was like I had struck a very valuable gem in the ground no one knew ever existed, I never knew existed. In celebration, I kept being a prospector for the unforeseen moments of laughter and light in every day.

In a hard day's work I could lay aside my shortcomings and defects and strike for gold and diamonds in drawing near to places where people laughed and cried and danced. Laughter was the element of spirituality I sought for a long time. Even the joy of making others laugh is important, and I wholly credit my father for setting this example.

Hugs and handshakes started to mean something for me. It was a miracle I could finally see my defenses break apart. There was no more threat, except the threat I created in my mind. I allowed it to take me over as if I had surrendered to another war.

As I grew more into my healing life and could examine myself clearly and in a healthy way, I saw how I had developed new masks to hide my more difficult emotions and thoughts. Trauma triggers us into going deep into ourselves in this way, and in some ways I realized at the time that if I didn't muster up the courage to face myself when I was presented with new challenges, I could easily fall apart. I'm thankful I still had that fear.

Once I was living on my own I began to realize my own power with thoughts and ideas, and I began to compartmentalize my life. I'd switch from one coping skill to another: thoughts, music, ideas, thoughts, self-awareness, fears, thoughts, food, sleep, daydreams.

I became particularly fascinated with heavy and deep topics: death, for example, again. Death has many facets and meanings. There is the literal sense of the word, and also the fact that feelings of loss can reach deeply into our psyche and our soul. In some form, deep down, we seek this mystery. We can't predict how or when we will meet our death. And we may create fears and false ideas about it. Every living thing dies. I see now that my trauma had been a major disruption in my emotional life.

Although I was too young at the time to understand what a physical death meant, in many ways the loss of my innocence at such a young age represented a similarly painful death, a difficult process of letting go. It didn't help me learn how to develop a healthy perspective of dying but it helped me create another "dual self" who replaced me in addiction. In some very distorted way I saw my acts of self–destruction as a tool to help bring meaning to death and dying. I created my other "self" in order to survive.

Human beings strive for ways to come to terms with their lives and learn to accept their mortality and death. I believe that life for every young soul was decided long before anything ever happened on the planet. It was decided as long ago as the first moments the sun coaxed the grass up through the earth. I can see my mind as having a birth and death to it, but never my consciousness.

Wounded Healer / Lee Lyttle

I have experienced many times the death of my mind through what I have learned, and what some others will call insanity. Through evaluating my thoughts and uncovering patterns, which was painful for sure, I know for certain that many of my difficulties now are self-perpetuating issues of thought stemming back to my ways of thinking. Being already an over thinker of sorts, I have learned that in my insane thinking I can easily overwhelm myself with my thoughts.

Starting to understand and reflect upon this issue of my duality opened up a whole new journey of self-awareness and discovery for me. This was healthy self–actualization, as American psychologist Abraham Maslow explained. I had been using my thoughts to navigate through decisions, reflections, imagination, creativity, problem-solving, contemplation, and dreaming.

I separated myself from my thoughts, which meant I was no longer dominated by them. However, another aspect of this duality was the existence of a maladaptive personality, a shadow that also sought out pleasure and comfort. This was problematic at times because I felt I was a pretender in my own life.

One day I felt I was experiencing intense imaginative and creative growth and the next I was conforming to man-made, laws, regulations, even morals, which I valued. I felt conflicted about always trying to fit in. It was important for me to sit in my own pain to avoid the world, but this was not what my soul wanted.

I needed to develop a non-conformist soul that also valued true justice and morals, maybe ones pertaining to balance and abundance and commonality and reciprocity, generosity.

One problem with being a non-conformist was that my behaviours were being heavily shaped by my moments of defensiveness, cynicism and, sometimes, hatred for the crueler aspects of mankind. Many times I grew jaded and my addicted self used this all to justify my own pain.

In recovery, when I finally got there, I had to learn to live my life in a full circle, accepting everything that landed in my sphere.

73

Breaking Through

Two things caused breakthroughs for me. Two different people in two separate incidences told me I had disappointed them, nothing major, however I noticed my response: I was gentle with myself, and did not blame myself, nor did I resent or blame others.

My thoughts of worry and shame or frustration were gone within 10 minutes. I responded with some kindness and humanness to my self. I used to always take ownership of other people's thoughts and reactions and ideas and feelings; they were not my own. I would become entangled in situations without fully being aware of, or listening to, warning signs within me. Or, when I started to see a natural warning sign, I felt uneasy and had few skills to navigate through what was going on.

Now I have new skills of tuning in to my warning signs, and I typically ask for help and guidance. I pray. I listen to what Nature is telling me. In my youth I was aware that many social circumstances were difficult for me, including every interaction with family and peers at school, and with teachers, store clerks, and bus drivers, as well as with people in positions of authority— even the crossing guard at Elizabeth Bagshaw Elementary School in Hamilton. They all represented an irrational threat to me.

I think if you or anyone you know has experienced trauma, addictions, or mental health issues, it is vital to do a thorough housecleaning of all your past relations as part of your healing process. I had to move past the fears and regrets I've had and, in particular, the harm I've done to others. However there is a pot of gold waiting for anyone who corrects these mis-steps from the past, who changes their behaviour or perceptions about what they thought was true.

Numerous self-examinations of my past have also given me accountability and responsibility. I've been able to shape how I wanted my interactions with people to unfold. I have been able to see and correct the places where I once had poor boundaries. Plus I've learned how to be respectful of my energy and this has tied into my understanding of the spiritual being that I am.

Wounded Healer / Lee Lyttle

A part of being a healthy person lies in recognizing our part in all of our interactions, and also in being honest about what we bring to our relationships. How we express our needs to others, and understanding how our instincts operate, are also important.

My Body

One of the frequent themes in my thinking as I aged was about my body and how I was functioning. I started to really sense my relationship with the world in a way I could understand, which was essentially through my physical being. I sensed I had a bone structure, some sections of flesh burning in madness, and a soul that desired to escape; and yet it was all *within* me.

I felt I was dying as I envisioned my old self, struggling on a narrow path, winding down toward a stream. My flesh hung onto me, with no consciousness, and no gut, and it sought isolation. I didn't have the power to tear my skin off, and so my imagination became my refuge. The language-processing part of my brain couldn't make sense of a single thing, yet my entire physical being had an underlying connection to life. I was curious about this. In psychological terms this is often referred to as compartmentalizing. I felt comfort would come through understanding the skills necessary for me to reach a minimum standard of survival in society.

Through therapy and constant exposure to my support groups, I learned to recognize other defense mechanisms, such as humour. Although taking care of myself physically was something I had never looked into when I was younger, I eventually created an overall healthy life through physical activity and trying to eat healthily.

When I was young I had developed some social anxieties that I simply could not work through, and the lack of certain social skills resulted in many failures and poor outcomes for others and for me. Physiologically we know more and more today, with new research coming out, as well, on the brain and trauma. This is an exciting time.

I just recently purchased the book, *The Body Keeps the Score* by Bessel Van Der Kolk, MD, and plan to read it soon. Many of my close friends in recovery have said highly positive things about it and I am confident it will help me discover some of the more healing aspects of my trauma.

I feel grateful even now that I am able to recognize earlier the small signals my body gives me when something is about to occur. This might be a pleasant feeling or a threatening one; it could be a simple "gut feeling" or a twitch in my right hand and arm. Perhaps that is how things manifest in me more or less as a preventive measure. The physical sensations alert my mental awareness to sort out whether the threat my body is perceiving is an irrational thought or a well-grounded one. And now, being the explorer of my own life experiences, I am actually excited to catch this new wave of psychology, spirituality and the behavioural sciences.

As part of this forming of the self I saw along my journey, I could not evade the fact that there was still a very powerful underlying drive for me to allow Nature and my sense of a soul to carry me through.

The Grace of Meditation

I've discovered that meditation is very helpful for me. I first heard about this practice indirectly while listening to the CBC radio show, "Brave New Waves," in around 1995 when I was finishing high school. The program featured a Tibetan Monk chanting and I closed my eyes, likely having seen this somewhere. Although I didn't totally understand this practice, I was intrigued.

After this experience, I started recording "Brave New Waves" episodes to capture more of the chanting and the various experimental sounds the program featured. In my own personal way I started by sitting with eyes closed in a quiet space with one or two lit candles. I can't explain it, but in some ways this brought some relief in the form of getting in touch with my mind and body.

Unfortunately, it wasn't enough to prevent my alcoholism from progressing at the time, and I wasn't introduced to the idea or practice of meditation again until years later when I was in Recovery and following the 12 Step program of Alcoholics Anonymous (AA).

The 11th step urges us to live our life so we can one day say we " Sought through prayer and meditation to improve our conscious contact with God *as we understood Him,* praying only for knowledge of His will for us and the power to carry that out."

My experiences with meditation since that discovery have been at times difficult to place into words as a deeper mysterious meaning has evolved as my practice has continued to unfold.

Equally important for me has been the desire to avoid the hokey-pokey societal ideas of meditation, and the spiritual "gurus" with suspicious financial motives who have taken the serious and valid practice of meditation and turned it into a lightweight fad.

I do know I often find great relief when I return to the pleasant visionary ability I have tapped into. Being drawn to vision, I've found that play and creativity keep my mind grounded and are one of the greatest medicines that have helped me to heal.

I have also grown to embrace meditative experiences, which engage all my senses of sight, sound, hearing, touch, and smell. They keep me grounded in my human journey.

During one particular meditation, as I approached the path which lay in the visual meadow of my mind, I realized I had the ability, when all else failed outside for me, to dig deep and discover a well of goodness that was sustaining and full of hope.

In meditative visions even today, I often return to that meadow. The path I tread winds down toward a stream. I sense I have some strength in my eyes; I can sense muscles of resilience in my being and my bones. In my mind a voice that I call my Captain guides me. It is a voice of reason, understanding, wisdom, and conviction.

But there are other voices, as well, and I sense the duality of my self that is comprised of the inner critic and the voice of self-compassion. These two voices co-exist in their own dialogue and conflict, whether I am involved or not.

For some time in my meditations, I worked at reaching the edge of the stream, which flows at a slow pace through that golden meadow. Tall grasses and willows, and maples, lean over portions of the stream I have formed in my mind. It is a place of comfort that I reach through meditation and contemplation, a place where I can burrow deep into a place inside.

Today, I realize that I had structured a system of refuge from my troubled mind long before I understood the more technical term we call resilience today.

Through childhood trauma, I fought and surrendered, often both in the same moments, to my life experience.

I learned to both protect and flee a self in the skin during the challenges I faced in my life, particularly during childhood. I began to see that pain was actually a warning sign and a motivator I could use to assist me to change, and not just a sign of a difficult emotion.

As I grew to be a more complex individual, I learned more intricate strategies to protect and flee the self that was my dual self, or what I call the non-soul. The dead self. I define this as the addict, or the part of the soul, that is sick.

Not once in my life did I see that, although my dying self was difficult, I was at one with this difficult self and they were not separate from me, although I desired this to be so.

I am at one with my dead self now. And with this change and death of a self has come the letting go of old ideas. In many ways the death of old ideas was difficult to accept. It entailed a transition of a psychic sort, an internal shifting of thoughts, and an awareness of rigid patterns of thinking. So after the dual self fades and dies, a new self is born.

78

Even today I continue to shift daily in my sense of who I am, and my visions and self–examination have grown deeper. I am finally having moments where I rest in the meadow, sunshine splashing my face and covering every surface of my surroundings. These new thoughts have filled in the empty spaces where my old thoughts used to be held. I am resting in my own vision and contemplation, a whole being at rest in all of the self I have been discovering.

In one particular experience in my early recovery from addictions, I sensed light falling down upon me. It didn't remove shadows, which I found strange; I was expecting complete relief.

This was a good and humbling lesson. I had to learn that not all self-examination was meant to be peaceful, that there would be, and will be, difficult times during the process, and that's okay. This was a comforting thought. It took away the pressure of the idea that self-examination always needed to be followed by peace of mind.

I had to learn to detach my trauma experience from any new moments of emotional pain and healing I might experience; I saw this as growth and it gave me a sense of normalcy

Meditative Visions

Through my visions and meditations, I often see blue and pink lights flowing from my belly as I sit near the stream. They flow towards the sky. The sky is filling up with my belly and my belly is filling up with the sky.

I can feel a wonderful sensation in my belly, the back of my head and my neck. What we typically call butterflies now become a constant flow of pleasure, more than my skin, bones, and blood have ever felt. It is releasing some pure form of my being. I don't think of how I am supposed to feel. I just am.

I hold my breath and sense this amazing human condition of breath. Years of believing I was a certain condition of hurt and constant pain and struggle begin to fall apart. I imagine the lights growing stronger as they leave my belly. There are flames and sparks, yellows, shades of orange and red. And below them a steady flame of blue and pink.

Suddenly I have new thoughts and ideas, and although I had thought that "nothing's going to change my world" I see new meaning in the words of John Lennon and Paul McCartney. I had been wrong. I was courageous and strong and this thought served to counter the pain and isolation of my life. It burned out in me through symptoms of anxiety, worry, and despair. My addictive mind had fought every single fight it could, but my soul burned through all that nonsense. My soul began to win.

As I continued to deepen my meditation practice, my visions increased, and my resilient self and my imaginative self began to completely tear away the addictive self which had been residing in me.

The disillusionment I felt at having been betrayed began to fade. I am becoming that which I seek. A new liberating force began to hold me to the ground and steady me. It was almost as if a written document was handed to my heart, a restraining order forbidding my old destructive self from ever setting foot in the doorway of my soul's porch again.

We all have demons and forms of despair, and hopelessness. I was now setting these aside more frequently, along with my strong and healthy inner critic, as new and profound experiences of transformation took hold.

I realized I had to accept my new consciousness. It was simple: I had a mind that constantly tried to seek pleasure and relief when I sensed even a little disturbance. This reflected the irrational and highly sensitive person I had become. It reflected a borderline insanity, if we can use that term. I don't throw that term around loosely. I can only share my experience with my own mind and thoughts.

It was important for me to see that I did not have the monster in my mind that I thought I had, that my thinking was the result of a conflict between my own personal defenses, the areas of resistance I myself was setting up and, ultimately, my own thoughts.

I knew part of my pain came from listening to my inner critic all the time, and it was a hard task to stop that because that voice was often loud and rude. Long years of therapy and support group work helped me learn how to reflect on ways in which my thinking was often incorrect.

Real change happened when I started to question my own inaccurate thoughts about my place in the world, and began to see things differently. I began learning about humility.

In the years since this passage in my life I have grown to understand the impact social labels have on disorders. I am not a qualified psychiatrist, but this is a very delicate and sensitive topic to discuss and during my years of recovery I had to be very careful about how I labeled myself. In the past I have completely (mis)diagnosed myself with a whole shitload of labels, not all of them true.

But I do believe I have experienced addictions to food, sex, alcohol, driving fast or driving fast cars, toxic or unhealthy relationships, athletics, overspending, big shot-ism, impulsive spending, caffeine, and romantic obsessions. I have consistently sought relationships with people who were unavailable.

Often obsessed with images of fantasy, I have been an ego-centric, egomaniac with an inferiority complex, and I have been a self-seeking, dishonest jackass at times, with the occasional severe personality problem. I'm an attention seeker who has struggled with paranoia, and perhaps social anxiety, and I've been diagnosed with generalized anxiety disorder, mild depression and distorted ideations of reality.

For good measure, throw in a complex sleep avoidant personality, an acute intimacy disorder and the fact that I'm co-dependent. I also love walks in the park and going for coffee and spending time with my dog, who happens to be the fastest wiener dog in Ontario. Generally, I'm a pleasant fellow to have around. I was laughing at myself when I wrote this and thinking how interesting it would be if it were my dating profile.

In the past, I didn't understand the nature of the deep emotional pain I experienced and I believe it was in those moments that my soul captured me. I felt as though my body was being tossed about in a sea and endless storms battered me in every moment. I couldn't drown, because Nature was right there waiting for me and I was grateful. I was grateful, too, when I realized that there was another sort of metaphysical element beyond mind and life, which protected my soul while I went through my healing journey.

It's not always easy to face the Universe when it arrives, for example through daily contact with others in recovery or others I met healing through trauma—it was tough to break through my denials that I was indeed very ill.

It was through honest conversations with others that I learned the truth and it hurt. I did not always like to see the truth, but as they say, it was a process of setting me free.

I've seen people in recovery appear to accept they were sick and some have spoken of how it was a relief to surrender and admit they were ill. Mentally and spirituality. Honesty became the biggest life skill I had to work on and I used it to chip away at the thick layers of denial with which 'd cloaked myself.

In some capacity I related Honesty with some form of Reality and in that Reality I started to see my world growing more open. This was the universe I saw I was becoming a part of. I knew my soul had some distant connection to it. To a truth perhaps. I began to feel and sense the power, creativity and meaning of my highly sensitive self. I had been lonely between the ages of two and 20.

The Universe had not abandoned me but rather had taken me to another dimension to protect me it until it was safe for me to live in my own soul, in my own flesh.

I began to trust that this new sense within me was having a profound impact on my psyche. No words can describe this; I honestly believe there are certain things that our human minds are not able to comprehend.

I believe that no matter how much science, research, and technology we have, and no matter how much knowledge we have of Nature, or how complex our language, laws, and principals are, or even how deeply we observe and account for our experiences, we are still unable to truly grasp and even begin to understand what lies beyond this life.

Visions and More Abstract Imagination

One winter night in 2014, while staying at a resort across the road from the seniors residence where my grandfather resided, I awoke from sleep knowing my grandfather was in his last stages of life, and unfolding before me was another profound experience...

Shaken to my bones, I trudged into the white hills; I pulled my legs up over the wooden fence surrounding parts of the Isaiah Tubbs Resort in West Lake Ontario. The yellow blood of the stars' light fell onto me. I began running and hopping. I look down and saw that part of my leg and my foot had morphed into a deer leg and a hoof. Fur covered my shins, and I continued to hop and step through the yellow stars. With my nostrils expanding rapidly I could see the breath inside me rushing out and creating shadows as my legs pressed into the snowdrifts. My shadow reflected on the banks. My imagination once again took hold and it was wild.

My breath continued to grow heavier and my voice started to come out, expressing my sense of the rawness of my being. The breathing was powerful and allowed me to fully sense my animal self as I jumped up and over the snowdrifts.

I sensed my grandfather's shallow breaths as he lay across the street. I had spent so many years of my life running from my entire being and now I craved the act of embracing it; in some mystical way my being lay in a building across the street.

This is the reality of experiencing real loss: it challenges you to question everything. I wanted and needed to connect to my grandfather, but the time available for that was leaking away from me.

I finally stepped onto a road near midnight.... I stood in the middle of the road and I turned to face east. In the distance I continued to sense and feel my grandfather's last breaths. In one short moment, reality tore into my chest, hitting me with my feeling of loss that forced me to dig away at examining my own physical self and even my mortality. I continued to walk for about 40 yards to the middle of the country road. It was the dead of night with no one else in sight. And then it happened. In a moment, I sensed about 100 beings, and energy and some transparency filling the street behind me.

They were reaching towards me and I knew that the body of a hundred souls was my home, blood and soul, all in one body of beings standing in purity waiting behind me. I could see out of my back and I saw the beings forming and dancing in a montage similar to the northern aurora, their wings—some torn—swept the light snow on the road's surface. I knew if I turned around, all the elements of me would vanish. So I held strong and took it in. I could feel light hit my lower back and cover my upper body. I knew I'd been missing from these beings for years. I felt like I was finally reaching a distant planet I'd been seeking for decades.

In that heightened state of sensitivity I asked what my relationship to these beings was. What was my relationship to "it?" The road remained quiet. A hundred forms still kept their distance, as though they were a massive ship waiting to dock. I was the pier, and they had been sent back to me...

The total outcome of my own grieving was that I sought more security in a Universe, or a Multiverse. This period or season in my life was very difficult for me as I was supporting my Grandparents' end-of-life care and supporting my mother through the loss of both of her parents.

I remember how important it was for me to be by my mother's side as she was grieving the loss of her own mother.

Many nights at the hospital I held my mother while she cried and at the same time reached out my hand to hold my grandmother's hand. As we all can relate and identify with this experience of life and beyond, it no doubt hits all of us at the very core of our being. And for me, the experience of sitting beside my mother while she cried, and watching my grandmother take her last breaths, prompted more internal reflection regarding my own path.

Big events like this force us to either flee or face and question our own existence and mortality. In my view, I believe this is one reason why many fall into a sort of shocked state when death occurs personally in our lives. It may not be so much that our loved one is gone, yet more of the questions arise that challenge our own beliefs and the meaning of our lives.

The Biggest Trigger

During further moments of reflection, I recognize I have wished for an end in my past; I have stood at that jumping off place, more than once. There was a growing shame of not having lived up to an ideal of my own life.

Death has probably been the biggest trigger for me that has prompted more searching.

It showed me how many times I had searched for a sign of life in me, yet I would run when I noticed a bit of light, which I now recognize as the light of acceptance. Maybe I couldn't consume it. Perhaps the light burned.

I believed in my core that if I eventually learned to deserve a light within me, it was not my responsibility to keep the flame going.

All I had to do was to know it was there and accept it was in me, always shining, although, on occasion, barely flickering. Then the duality would set in.

During these same moments of truth I felt disgusted by all the muckiness I saw, or that I believed was surrounding that light. I believed in my light, yet I also believed I was deeply defective.

My soul is a very patient soul. Patience, to me, is the condition of the soul. It's seen me and allowed me to fail. Allowed me to participate in the moon's rising and falling.

I was evolving into a new master of my mind standing on the edge of new mysteries. I was studying my blood and my bones. My seeking does not end and never will, because the Multiverse also seeks me.

I'd never before considered Nature wanted to spend time with me. It wasn't until the absence of my confused self that I began to discover the powerful existence of something wonderful inside me and faced the undeniable existence of what truly was animating me, and accept that existence without protest.

I began to recognize that my dual self was nothing more than an illusion whose only purpose was to feed those black wolves of my active life through addictions and character flaws.

There were times I'd given up on my life and it's difficult now to see I'd attempted suicide many times, sitting on the kitchen floor, intoxicated, with a knife pressed against my chest, almost as if I needed to cut out the deep pain within me. I am truly grateful that can now provide that important love and caring for myself.

Things really started to fall into place when I saw that this memoir itself was the exact shaping of my story, that my life was occurring again, taking on a new existence that was shaped through my words, and it was happening without much of my own intent effort.

It reinforced my faith in beliefs that took decades to confirm and gave me a purpose to ensure my voice was heard.

A Long Winter's Poem

In my quiet moment

Resting here in the bay

A reflection so majestic of the snow scape in the Raven's eyes.

Is he weary, I inquire?

He and I have been swimming in the ocean grey

My love turns to the shadow of the wing

There it is, the dark point of his wing

Wild in its form touching the edge of the winter sky

Atop the surface of the shadows

We are born alike

We are not concerned for the setting of the sun

Because there is a fire in our veins

The same fire beneath my skin

The wings bump and jump on the drifts,

The creator of new winds.

I am born into this moment and it feels so good.

My new warmth.

I see the Raven's wings burning from the stars within his belly

Atop my shoulders, my breath, my rush

A process of madness and hunger fills my spine

We are both lifted to gather the fire from the stars

In love with this world.

I sit on his back as we fly through the galaxy

As we approach the tree line

Wounded Healer / Lee Lyttle

Below we see a white fox and he is waving his paw

The Raven quickly plucks a small twig and holds it in his beak

New colors of pink, blue, and yellow are forming on his coat as I grip and hold tight

I am still resting

In a raspy voice he sings out to me in song

Calling us both captains of patience

The beauty of this land has broken down my entire humanness

I am humble.

As we set for the sun, he directs me to scoop a small flame from its surface with the twig

I then place the twig with a flame back into his beak

In a reflection I notice his eye turning and forming to a dark pupil

I see the land below breathing deeply up and down as we approach,

The swamps beneath the frozen surface are breathing, too, and swaying, much like the floor of an ocean,

Like frozen grass caught in the northern Arctic winds.

Slowly landing I am left floating off the back of the Raven and I begin to sleep under a small bush.

I am barely awake and I see in the distance the Raven handing the twig with fire over to the small fox.

And I fall asleep again against the snowdrift without fear

As I have a coat of stars keeping me warm.

4 Hitting Bottom and Recovery begins

In my early twenties I hit bottom and for four years I lived alone before ultimately beginning my recovery journey back from alcoholism.

What did bottoming out look like? One day, in the summer of 1996, while alone in my apartment in Hamilton I lay on the floor of my living room admitting I was done, and physically sick and in withdrawal from a heavy few days of drinking.

I knew I was about to break and fall apart, but for the first time, I felt safe. A marathon of Charlie Chaplin movies was playing on the TV. Watching 10 hours of Chaplin brought great comfort to me: I needed some smiles and humour to undermine the deep sorrow I had felt for years.

I slept off and on that day, waking up sweating, and in fear I crawled around on the floor, sometimes flipping and tossing, until I cried once again and fell asleep.

After sleeping for quite some time, maybe even a day or two, I woke up to feelings of renewal. The first thing I noticed was that my breathing was different. It was new. I

looked out the window of my little Kenilworth apartment in east Hamilton and I saw a man crawling drunkenly along the sidewalk near the pub across the street. When he turned his face, I was frightened, as I saw my own face, saw myself on my hands and knees, pathetic and incapable.

I started to see conflicts and contradictions in myself that I finally had a chance to examine. I needed strength and faith to examine this. I was to feel a new discomfort as I learned to trespass against my own delusion and dishonesty. God brought me to a place of safety where I could finally be with myself. But I wasn't finished with bottoming out.

A little later, in the summer of 1996, I was at a concert in Brockville, Ontario, listening to April Wine and Blue Rodeo with my mother and my grandparents. When Blue Rodeo played the song *Dark Angel*, I was hit with fright and panic. I'd been drinking heavily that night on my own. I strangely remember feeling a calm acceptance and peaceful feeling as though I would be happy if I drank myself into death.

And somehow I ended up wandering around Brockville. I recall standing on a bridge in heavy contemplation about ending it all. I was feeling deep sadness and fear and shame. Shaking uncontrollably I recall my knees wanting to walk up the side of the railing but I was also holding my own arms down. I thought, If my body shut down my shame would end. I knew it was a short fall but if I timed it right to hit a train or dove so my head would smash against the railing, it would be quick. I was gasping and crying and also blacking in and out. I dropped to my knees and passed out for a few minutes Along with the deep sadness, shame and remorse, I started to feel a sense of giving up, but in a different way. I felt I had no power in me to make a choice. I believed again, as I had for so long, that I was destined to die. Later on I found this was more of a core belief that I believed I was never really meant to live life at all. How false this belief was!

I called and cried to the sky. And something happened. In my spiritual learning, I simply call this Divine Intervention. Something held me back from stepping off the edge. Ultimately, a single courageous thought entered my mind. Perhaps in my drunkenness there was a ray of hope and I continued to stumble my way home. The next thing I knew I woke up on the couch at my grandparents' place. It took me about a week to feel like I was starting to recover from the booze and sickness, and the onset of depression and anxiety accompanied by the intoxication.

It wasn't until the fog cleared in my mind that I sensed the strengthening of the thought of being willing to live this life. It was new. Also new was my willingness to do what I had to do to take care of my health. I felt different, as if many fears of living fell from my shoulders. I saw something to grab onto in the wind like a life coat and in desperation I held on.

90

It wasn't until later in my recovery from alcoholism and trauma that I learned from others in the recovery field that we may actually hit many bottoms in our lifetime, more importantly emotional bottoms. I learned I needed to see these bottoms as not so much a threat, but as a healthy change because essentially deep painful moments can lead us to better places. I should not be surprised that other moments of pain will arise in my life

I needed to be taught the hard lessons of discipline, spiritual obedience, and self-control, and the outcome of this learning, eventually, was self-acceptance and self-love. I needed to see with clarity the consequences of my decisions, to see my path of self-destruction. How immoral I was, how sick I had become.

Facing this sickness was the ultimate remedy for me. I knew all that pain I held in was starting to pour out and in many ways I felt a great freedom.

The pain strikes hardest when we recognize how we've created so many masks to wear in an effort to avoid the pain we know still sits inside us. Then there's the additional pain of realizing the truly selfish motives we've had. I have learned that my words are powerful. I have to be careful, and think about what I'm saying. I have to really watch my motives and watch for manipulation when I am in fear. This causes anxiety.

I am not an addiction expert, nor am I a psychologist, a psychiatrist, or a spiritual healer. I do not speak for 12-Step support groups or have any opinions on the actual therapy I've done in my life. God forbid that anything should happen to me as a result of my addictions—I want readers to know that when I relapsed it was not a failure of therapy or the 12 Steps, but a disaster of my own making.

At the point at which I felt tempted to end my life on that Brockville bridge, I'd been receiving formal therapy and had attended thousands of Alcoholics Anonymous (AA) meetings for two years from 1996-1998. During this time I'd done pretty much everything the elder members had suggested. The old script says, "Join a group, get active, get a sponsor." Which I did.

I heard an AA speaker once describe first coming into the AA fellowship as like the Blind Melon video "No Rain," in which a girl dressed in a bumble bee outfit finally at the end of the video reaches a field of bumble bees and she is no longer alone. I can totally identify. Sadly the amazing artist Shannon Hoon, lead singer of Blind Melon, committed suicide in 1995.

Having said that, all of my crucial experience with hitting bottom and beginning this path of healing were, in my view, a divine intervention. Whether the reader here wishes to interpret the process of change from a religious, spiritual, or science-of-human-behaviour perspective, I'm open to any feedback. This is simply my experience. To me, it's none of the above.

When I first entered the world of recovery from alcohol in 1996 I was aware I was drinking alcohol heavily, to the point where I felt I didn't want to wake up. I thought I was too frightened perhaps to end my life in drastic ways, and I knew I could probably just drink enough alcohol in one night to get the job done for me. As for my physical health, two or three days of drinking would cause me to endure serious vomiting episodes and shakes, in addition to paralyzing social fears, and fears about my own thinking and sanity. I recall even having intense flashbacks related to past trauma while I was in withdrawal, and anxiety.

In reality, I think I was done. Deep inside I wanted to live, yet I was confused and young. Some relationship problems served as a crisis that motivated me to start attending Alcoholics Anonymous meetings in the Hamilton area, and I attended from 1996-2000. I completely immersed myself in this new family and I know I felt I was getting the emotional, moral and mental support I needed in life. And I hung on for dear life.

I began attending many AA 12-Step meetings in Hamilton and Southern Ontario. I felt good and started to feel like I was taking care of my health. Sometimes, I would attend three or four meetings a day, and I also began to get more deeply involved in 12-Step recovery, joining groups and volunteering within the AA service. I think I did many things in meetings to keep busy because it helped my mind.

I also volunteered my time sharing my story at Youth Detention Centres and Hamilton Detention Centre. I mopped the floors, cleaned tables and made coffee. People would tell me I had a story to share. I felt there was a very deep therapeutic value to meeting others with similar life struggles. We all seemed to belong to a common force, which was actively seeking a common purpose, to live a good quality of life, even though it was going against another part of our character, which was to run and vanish.

Meaningful Exchanges

Regular attendance at AA meetings helped me build a circle of loving, non-judgmental folks who accepted me. It was meaningful for me to share with others about my alcohol and drug addictions and my suicide attempts.

I spent some time going into youth detention facilities in Hamilton to share my story. The more I spoke with complete honesty, the more comfortable I felt about who I was. So my mind and spirit grew more and more hungry for learning about me as a person and felt a great sense of purpose I'd never felt before. This was the type of social skills training I needed, and enabled me to be a part of a shared experience. Fellowship with human beings was crucial for me. For the first time I could see that human interaction was a life line for me. The experience then—and to this day—has taught me how to be my own parent when I need to be.

I started to develop thinking skills that I believed the average person already had, such as knowing that when my thoughts or emotions were moving into a difficult area, I could trust myself, and examine them. I had never previously known what it was like to trust myself, and it felt good. I remember having many late-night conversations with other AA members about our thinking and we were all struggling with the same type of challenges relating to our thoughts. This thinking capacity grew as I questioned and talked honestly about what was happening inside me. Again my capacity to trust my thoughts showed me that this was a sign of recovery.

Early in my recovery my good friend, George C., told me that being confused is actually a sign of growth, because it means I am contemplating and expanding, and usually confusion is the sign of reaching new territory. I started to see the things that were difficult in life as lessons, rather than triggers for wallowing in self-pity or creating avoidant behaviour.

Once I began to become healthier, I realized there were many difficult things I had to accept about myself. I discovered more and more how broken being sexually abused had made me feel, and I also began to realize how much harm and damage I have caused others. Although the damage I have caused others at times through my behaviours has been great, I have made attempts to repair them and make amends. I try to make a conscious decision each day to give back to life and be responsible.

As both a progressive process and a path to follow, I believe Recovery calls us to learn to accept aspects of ourselves slowly, to avoid a complete breakdown of becoming aware too quickly of our unhealthy patterns. I am grateful that other people in Recovery told me that it takes time, and also that it is most often a lifelong process. I am grateful I decided early on to be content with the fact that I was unlikely to get quick relief from my troubles. That helped me avoid going back into the "real world" to survive. I realized that learning about myself in a new way, although frightening, was a better option than running away and avoiding responsibility.

Along with more insight into myself came more difficulties when I started to really see distorted thinking patterns, character "defects", or flaws. Some defects were more severe than others, including personality problems, and even behavioural problems where I would attempt to seek ease from other unhealthy activities, such as food, or sex and unhealthy relationships.

My new survival not only included abstinence from alcohol or drugs, but an ongoing awareness of unhealthy behaviours that, if left unchecked, might have led me back to the bottle.

In many ways each person in recovery is on their own unique path. I used to say, "what works for me, may not work for you and that is okay." But sometimes people in the Recovery world become dogmatic about their process, which can only do more harm than good, as it may prevent a person from finding ways to discover their own truth.

I worked hard and began to see my efforts to change were having a healthy impact on me. I felt it was important to keep myself safe. So what did I do when confronted with all the other underlying issues I was starting to discover? I had enough courage and love for myself that I knew I needed professional help. I worked with therapists, took CBT group therapy and counseling through anxiety disorder clinics, and at the same time tried to keep an open and honest dialogue with my AA friends and sponsors.

I also met people from Six Nations of the Grand River Reserve also on a path of recovery from alcohol. They invited me to Ceremony. I was taught lessons in Native Traditional Healing, for which I'm grateful, and honoured to have been invited.

In addition to exploring the childhood trauma part of my being, I attended a few adult male survivor groups to enhance my healing. Sometimes I was so numb from all the therapy processes that I couldn't even grasp what was happening, yet I knew if I brought my body, my mind would follow one day.

But what I also discovered through recovery health was that, although the mind and sanity are essential for health, my emotional well-being was what I really needed to cultivate and nourish as it would sustain me more powerfully than my mind.

Taking More Risks

There was a time in therapy, though, where I began to feel like it was time for me to take more risks and experience life. So, just like when I had to evolve my participation in my Recovery and 12-Step programs and learn to become my own parent, I had to start to detach from therapy and the security it provided. Having said that, I know I will always have that security to fall back onto, if ever I feel I am losing touch with my supports.

I do have to be careful to ensure I don't stray too far from them, as my mind tends to try to convince me that I am 100% okay. But all in all, I believe effective therapy, healing, and recovery are meant to bring us to a point where we go on and live life, perhaps the way we are intended to. I continue to embrace my life and recovery as a kind of an adventure and a documentary. This has always been my saving grace when times get tough.

I formed some strong connections by listening and sharing my life with other like-minded folks within the 12-Step Recovery groups. I've also formed healthy bonds outside my recovery circle. My ideas of the 12-Step fellowship have changed and my experience has evolved. Primarily I feel this exposure was the foundation I needed. It was a kind of spiritual kindergarten and the groups acted as a parent. Like any parent-child relationship there came a time when I had to grow up and practice what I had learned in real life. The beautiful part of this is that I have such trust, and have created so many healthy relationships with others, that I know that when I am straying away and feel like I'm getting lost, I can always call on my friends and my sponsor.

Addictions and mental health are hot topics now, more than ever, and I will say this to the reader: if you are struggling with uncertainty or recognize some aspect of yourself in my experience, be open to seeking and accepting assistance. We are not always aware of our deep need for change. My transformations and change were essentially engineered beyond my own efforts. Although I certainly set up certain structures and took action in my life—such as therapy appointments, numerous AA meetings, numerous self-compassion retreats, and even my academic ventures – it was ultimately the Creative Force that helped me determine what I was ready to tackle.

Currently in my life I have what I call a recovery routine where I've maintained health through prayer, meditation and the service work I do in life to give back. One major service to life and purpose is of course my career, which I'm grateful for, even with difficult moments.

I feel I've built up some "insurance," and I continue to make deposits into my bank by cultivating my relationship with God and others to the best of my ability.

Certainly life will blow me some heavy things. And that's when I need to put that extra effort again into seeking strength.

All in all my recovery and healing has been difficult and painful and many times I did not think I was going to make it. I know deep inside that if I were to drink again, I honestly don't feel I would last long on this Earth. That's a healthy fear.

I have tools now that I carry with me and they're called Honesty and Prayer. I get lost in the love of others around me and life and I simply feel the pain inside go away. I feel that in some ways God teaches me with more gentleness than He ever has before. I suppose I am learning greater discipline, but I only need to ensure I keep my pride in check and remain humble. Now I pray that I can keep close to God daily.

My understanding of the 12 Steps has been nothing more than a stepping stone to develop more faith and understanding. I see the recovery experience in AA as the one fundamental tool that's in my toolbox. I'm grateful that I've been able to incorporate my recovery from alcoholism into my work and career, although I've had to be very sensitive, as not everyone needs or wants to live a life of recovery in AA. Many people I know have started a recovery or healing life without self-help or counseling.

Education as Contact with the Living World

In the past few years I've realized I've always had some difficulty with structures and people who were in positions of authority, so much so that even the word has had an emotional impact on me. It took me a while to figure out what that was all about, but eventually I realized this was due to my early childhood trauma.

Since moving to Northern Ontario it's become clear to me that throughout most of my life my unconscious mind has been seeking a deeper understanding of what the idea of "authority" meant to me, and what it had to teach me. Today, it's interesting to that my work and academic experiences have shaped an aspect of my personality that does, in fact, have an authoritative aspect to it. I've been consistently drawn to a position in life where I'm asked to be a leader and this has been very grounding for me.

This authority in me has brought a new confidence lit by humility and integrity. The authority in me is a tool to ensure I can use my voice in a just way. This inner authority is the voice of my inner child. It's the regaining of the power of the innocence I lost many years ago. It's the changing of my perspective to believing in peace and good direction. Peace and innocence have more power than anything else I've known in life. And this was growing inside me all along.

My studies have emphasized the fact that becoming comfortable with and conversant in silence is very difficult for most people. I think of my own silence, of how I searched for many years for silence in my heart and mind. Most importantly, of how the many transformations I have experienced have resulted from living many years in my head. I needed to accept that true health for me came when I started to see my thoughts turn to actions, practice and application.

Over the past two years of working in child welfare I have come to realize that I used to be somewhat frightened of the idea that I myself had a sense of authority that I could exercise and practice. Yet all along this is exactly what I was trying to develop.

I suppose I had been worried about the word "authority" and focused too much on the authority other people and systems had. This blinded me to the fact that I myself had a deep authoritative voice inside me which was trying to speak. I suppose I was always trying to see myself as a gentle man, which is true, and for the most part I know I am content with life. And I rarely— if ever—get angry or aggressive. In the past I think I was always more angry with myself, and turned that anger inward in shame.

Over the past few years I have recognized the power I myself hold and, quite frankly, I believe this idea initially frightened me, because I wasn't sure how I would handle it. Also, I was uncertain how people would respond when they start seeing me handling my own power and practicing it. I thought I might fall into false pride or, knowing my ego, take this power beyond its best intended use.

Then in meditation I saw I could still behave with authority and be gentle at the same time. I began to grow, and I become confident that there was some space inside me to hold other qualities necessary for building character and thriving. This to me is more like realizing that I have integrity.

Thank God for my experience with my work life and my academic life because, this has always taught me how I can discover, develop and cultivate integrity both professionally and personally. Education, to me, has had one major purpose: to acquire the knowledge I need to set my own boundaries and set boundaries for others. Education is sort of a rule for social survival.

In many ways, as well, there has been another education of searching and discovering myself: this is an education without any certificate, as the unfolding of my life is ongoing. Coming to respect my memory is perhaps my greatest achievement, yet it hasn't brought me a piece of paper that acknowledges the hard work it takes to heal from childhood trauma. Learning to accept my day-to-day conditions is also my certificate for reaching on-going levels of health.

After high school I worked hard at odd jobs as a labourer. I took some pride in working hard and I've had some jobs which were very physically taxing and in rough conditions.

One day, someone suggested I get into a helping field, like social work. I had never really considered it, but I've always loved learning, so away I went. I started with exploring various part-time courses at McMaster University in Hamilton Ontario, most of them related to anthropology. I valued the sense of how seeking knowledge, and walking around the McMaster Campus, and sitting in the old buildings brought me a sense of peace.

Then, I applied for Mohawk College and graduated with a Social Service Worker diploma. This led me into working at the Salvation Army Booth Centre, which was a men's homeless shelter in Hamilton, Ontario.

Sharing stories and meeting people who were living in the constant agony of poverty, loneliness, despair, addictions, and serious untreated mental health issues motivated me more to learn and work more.

In about 2005, I landed a job as a therapist for acquired brain injury, which proved to be another experience, which was an essential part of shifting my career into the helping profession. I felt grateful to have opportunities to be exposed to experiences that would develop my intellect and acquire more knowledge.

Earlier in my life I had known that the seeking of knowledge represented a way for me to provide myself some relief, as it helped my mind feel as if it belonged in some aspect of the life I saw around me. As I mentioned earlier, I sought this intelligence, but being selfish and afraid, it was all for the purposes of maintaining my ego.

Now, I could see where I could have an opportunity to really becoming functional in life. I turned my brain into a kind of sponge.

Education in life and academics, and real life experiences which did not involve trauma, kept me connected to the world then, and they still do today. This is something I value.

My learning spirit has also helped me with my own inquiry into and curiosity about my own self. I question everything, and I'm sure some people today would get very annoyed at my incessant need to analyze things.

But education has enabled me to work away at finding a new language and it's called critical thinking. I am learning now that many of my communication problems with others has resulted from the fact that critical thinking has not been encouraged in our world. It doesn't mean I am more intelligent or "better" than anybody in any way; it just means that I find people sometimes lack basic communication skills. They don't listen, can't communicate and never challenge themselves about their own beliefs.

I believe my hunger for working hard was partly a gift of genetics, with my father instilling a good solid work ethic in me. Working hard made me feel proud and helped me face many employment situations head on; I would roll up my sleeves and jump right in to get the work done.

The Stories We Share

Our very lives are shaped by the simple little stories we share, and certainly having a new understanding of my own stories, I am more interested now in the stories of other people.

I understand the first universities in England were formed around the study of philosophy, critical thinking, arts, and sciences. Education was meant to teach young people to think critically about the world and themselves.

Now education seems to be focused on materialism, business and technology. Hence we see fewer people actually exercising good thinking skills in terms of our human nature, and imagination seems like an old lost art.

To me, education is essentially about telling stories. The indigenous population looked at talking and listening as a technology. Now, our modern technology in some respects has eliminated the original technology of communication and listening.

I was taught during my own early recovery from alcoholism and mental health issues, that recovery forbids us from thinking we have control or power. Part of this philosophy is the idea that our best thinking, and our best efforts at staying sober, actually did nothing more than get us drunk. So our own thinking resources doom us.

The AA program supports the idea that we have to make efforts to work away at getting our thinking right but we must be cautious as our thinking tends to be heavily linked to self–will. This makes sense intellectually to me due to the fact most of my difficulties were born out of self-centredness, selfishness, and ego.

However, I feel I also needed to start to experience a sense of being in balanced control of my life, within a context that also included spiritual guidance. This is a very normal skill for the average person, yet for me, it takes just a little longer.

I struggled at times with the thought of generating any type of success in my life, although socially I was thriving deep inside as a result of some strong achievements. At times I did not feel worthy of my achievements. I resonate with the term "imposter syndrome."

Things began to turn around for me when others shared with me that they actually do not see me as having an ego or false pride. More and more I was able to see the inaccuracies in my own thinking. The more scientific term for this is "cognitive distortion." I have a deep and honest respect for this power within me. I have almost learned to sit and accept aspects of myself related to making my voice known and my story loud.

The force of my voice is the very purpose of this memoir and my ultimate purpose for, and service, in reaching others, specifically those who've experienced childhood sexual abuse.

Although this has been a healing journey for me, my hope is that this service of words may help others feel that whatever experiences you are having with life, you can come to a point where you embrace each day.

I want to show through my sharing that it is possible for anyone to dig away at whatever barriers, masks, or paralyzing fears you have and allow it all to lead you to your own voice and the discovery of your own story.

People shine when they are truly interacting with compassion and love towards one another.

5   Intimacy and Connection

Before I really began to seek connections with others, I didn't know it was simply okay to ask them to build a bridge to meet me halfway. I always believed I had to put in all the work in a relationship. This was extremely maladaptive. My whole life strategy was to avoid vulnerability and pain, avoid my fears of abandonment, and even avoid my responsibility for my life.

When I think of the way I was, I realize I have missed out on crucial parts of life. I realize how the trauma had affected me and how it has taken me an extra-maximum effort in order to move forward. In the past, this led me to believe that my life would not be as good as I thought it was meant to be. I began to see also that through healing from trauma and recovery I was building a new belief system around "asking for help"

While in recovery I heard someone say to me, "you know you just came back from death." When I finally heard that comment crystal-clearly, I realized how seriously I had separated myself from Life. The greatest connections for me were with the trees and the sky and the water. This connection is okay, but only to a point, as I discovered I was still hungry for a deep connection with others and I knew this was a common human need.

I often found that as I was drawing close to people, it felt to me as though they were getting too close to me, These moments occurred mostly during holiday events and birthdays. I recall an uneasy feeling of being lost and didn't feel I deserved the attention I was getting, or I was angry at myself when I saw people experiencing joy when I could not. I understand this now as a deep sense of unworthiness at work in the core of my being. I did not develop skills to regulate my emotions, and I could not see this was a possibility for me. So I froze up. I didn't know what safety was.

Today, I realize how essential connections with people are in my life. Despite all the events and trauma and destruction in my life, I have still had a deep need to feel trust and vulnerability, and this, to me, is true intimacy.

I now know that the unconscious and avoidant behaviours I had practiced—which had prevented me from getting close to people in the physical, emotional, mental, and, perhaps, spiritual realms—are very common among people who have suffered childhood abuse.

In my childhood, trustworthy adults held me, kept me warm, and even said kind words to me—in particular my many aunts and uncles on my father's side of the family. I recall my mother and father and family members telling me they loved me, missed me, and loved having me around. I know they probably sensed I felt lost and unworthy, because after a while one simply cannot hide this.

Many people did provide opportunities for me to flourish, and maybe they did help my development and even give me a real sense of confidence, yet I could not hang on to it. I recall how a teacher in grade school gave me the responsibility to monitor halls, although she must not have known what nonsense kids in Grade 4 can get up to. Apparently a small riot broke out but I must have felt a sense of responsibility and my good behaviour paid off: I was awarded some gold stars.

Yet, as I grew, the deep feelings of unworthiness always won out. I think in many ways I learned to stay in a kind of misery and it became addictive because it was the only feeling I knew I could hold when I was alone. I could not seed and nourish real intimacy; I lacked communication with others simply because I lacked communication and trust with myself.

In most of my relationships I would play the victim. I wanted to stay sick because I felt I needed to be that way, to be constantly seeking and needing nourishment. After much healing, I can see now where others provided security and compassion by taking me aside and talking with me.

My aunt Cathryn often sat down with me and tried to listen. I can recall many other relatives taking time to sit and be with me and even until this day my aunts and uncles and family still show me love, and I am grateful for that.

I recall an incident where I was having a fight with a cousin and my father disciplined me by telling me to go and apologize to my grandmother for fighting in front of her. Now, after working away at this memoir, I can truly start to appreciate the good people who were in my life to protect me. My aunts and uncles from Alberta always held me and hugged me, even now I can remember hearing my aunt Kathleen and Aunt Christine talking with me, and holding me.

On one occasion I recall there was a crisis in the family and my grandmother held me and sat me on her lap when I cried. I've always remembered how important that was for me. I suppose I felt great shame for many years, as to why I may have felt those protective incidences still could not reach the main core of bringing relief to my pain.

Feeling Lost

Through numerous failed relationship attempts, I went through a variety of difficult emotions and experienced a general feeling of being lost.

I decided to order and build a shed for the back yard in the home I rented in Dundas, Ontario. Around this time, I found a card in a book that my Aunt Sonya gave me. There was no special occasion for the card, but it read "You are Loved."

In honour of the shed I completed, and my new hopeful days ahead, I pinned the card on the inside door and I took a moment to take in this experience of being loved. An immensely joyful innocence grew in my belly and rose up to my shoulders and neck. I stepped into my back yard still walking in this radiance, as if in a trance, with the green lawn shadowed by a row of cedars. The sunshine followed me into this moment of being loved. This is where another deep understanding of spirituality began to be formed.

I honestly believe certain people were placed in my life for a reason, and although I was unreceptive to their kindness, I still had to put in extra effort to trust them. I was resentful of that, and I blamed the world for placing me in this shit show.

I often asked myself why I could not feel things, why I could not hear things or see things as they really were. I could not express any feelings about anything physical in my life: I did not have the language to do so. Trusting my current circumstances, over time, enabled me to find ways to ground myself when I felt I was in full flight.

It helped once I could trust, even a little. The problem with having a crazy sophisticated emotional antenna was that I could sense harm from distances, and this prevented me from forming bonds and attachments. I was a fucking pro at keeping others at a safe distance. This, I have learned, is a very common characteristic of Survivors. This was my defense. The best defense is a good offense, right?

Yet, when others I was allowing to get close to me started to challenge me and call me on my bullshit, things got real. I knew I could no longer hide in my own self-sabotaging despair. I had to start accepting that, although I'd gone through trauma, I was causing myself more trauma by hiding in victimization. And, even though I tried harder and harder to hide, the love I was trying to give to myself was becoming more powerful.

I came to realize I had missed crucial developmental moments but that I had the power to provide those missing parts through correct love channeled through daily meditation and self-compassionate mindful practice.

During the disillusionment years of my life I was lost, living in a body with a brain that hadn't developed well enough yet to meet the realities of the world. I felt isolated because my life wasn't turning out the way I thought it was meant to. I had daily thoughts of suicide and hid them really well. The victim narrative in my life that I had created affected all my interactions with others. It was hard for me to come to terms with the harsh reality that I was sick and different.

But, eventually, I accepted myself for the person I was. I knew I had some brokenness to me, but I wanted to get healthy. I worked up the courage to walk into the Anxiety Treatment and Research Clinic at St. Joseph's Healthcare Hamilton, where a psychiatrist asked me, "What, are you afraid your brain is broken?" This challenged me on many fronts but I understood what he was getting at. I had to change my narrative about being a broken person. I started to see that I was and am not, in essence, my brain.

For the first time I could adopt a different perspective. I will always be grateful for those early therapy sessions where professionals challenged my inaccurate thoughts.

At the time, I was overwhelmed with trying to build a healthy imagination, and a vision for life, trying to balance reality and fantasy at the same time. This had so many consequences that I was often detached from reality and, also, from the emotional pain I was feeling; I did not want to do the work necessary to meet up with reality.

How were people ever going to help me if I didn't let them know I was hurt? That sentence is the single most important collection of words I've ever said in my life.

Having become a pro at sensing others' motives, I also started to see the real personal struggles they encountered, and this is when I started to develop empathy. I believe that ultimately led me into choosing a career in a helping profession.

Intimacy was Difficult

Intimacy was difficult because I knew at my core that I wanted to be loved, and I felt I couldn't trust my fleeting thoughts; I knew deep inside that others would have difficulty understanding me, so I formed a defensive system of always criticizing myself before others could criticize me.

What's strange is that others truly loved me and accepted me, but because I was hurting and sick, I couldn't accept myself.

Now I see how others talked kindly about me and practiced love and acceptance of me, but at the time I only saw where people had hurt me, or what I perceived to be hurt. This changed when people who loved me would not give up on me until I could start to love myself. They were the riverside branches and underwater boulders I could grab onto in the turbulent river passages where the flow was unmanageable for me.

From what was once an inability to form connections grew my awareness of the fragility of other human beings, and to finally understand that even those who had what I saw as success in life had breakdowns and doubts like I did.

My capacity to trust others only grew when my inner capacity to trust myself grew. I had always felt I was an imposter, but I was forced to be an interpreter of my world and that's where I began to over-think things.

I did not have the education to become an interpreter of another language, the language of living in a trauma-filled body, and make it jive with real experiences. And although I learned, my path was uneasy because my thinking was often distorted.

I was often trying to control my behaviour and although I often felt I was in control, at the onset of any anxious thought I fell, in a split second, right into severe moments of insecurity.

It's been a long journey to form my own, new ideas about my years from childhood to adulthood and, understandably, it's been hard work. Most of this difficult work has been around building healthy, secure attachments.

When I think of forming and shaping healthy attachments now, I know I need to ensure I am able to secure my emotions by self-compassion and self-love.

I need to recognize when I need to return to my heart and return to my thoughts in a non-judgmental or un-self-critical way.

I am now learning that I experience events and moments of self–awareness similar to those that others experience. And the meaning of these experiences is growing deeper over time.

Many times I tried desperately to accept myself as I was. I've learned that addiction and mental unwellness are symptoms of a greater illness, which is loss, or the inability to connect with people.

I've always said I love being in Nature and learning from Nature, but now I see more and more that for me to develop a healthy life, I also need to truly feel connected to others.

In some sad way I've also thought that being abused at a young age may have benefited me because I hadn't had a lot of time to develop a sense of connection that would have then been lost through the experience of abuse. I never really had a strong sense of innocence to begin with. This may still confuse me, because I still struggle with trying to build a new sense of innocence in my life, yet now, I'm, like, "fuck what if I lose that too?" I get angry that the world didn't provide for me the innocence I needed to develop and thrive when I was young.

I had to develop new ways of survival because I still could not begin a full healing process while immersed in deep pain. Now I can see that I have tapped into a world much bigger than my fears.

One area of major breakthrough for me in my healing journey came from something called Self-Compassion Mindfulness. I had seen a poster advertising a program about it at a Starbucks restaurant in Dundas one year and I registered. I thought, "Man, self–compassion. That is what I need, and I can add it to my existing toolbox of therapy techniques and practices." This practice would ultimately be the most effective one for me simply because it helped me learn the skills to really look at my pain and my detachment from life without having the wind knocked out of me. It helped me become completely in love with the person I am, not in an egotistical way, but in a healthy way.

109

Throughout my experience of reflecting on intimacy and connection, I have actually had visualizations of my heart and its presence within me:

I saw in my meditation one day

That my heart was a place I could return to

This place was safe and full and had never really been explored

This place had a space that was already created

Beyond any power I have ever known

There is a sacredness that keeps me going back to this place

My love for my heart is truly a scared moment

I see this place as secure with self-love

I am returning to my heart

I am returning to my thoughts without madness

Space is being created beyond my power

A new sacredness brings it back

You see, my shadow. I'm going to miss you, old friend

I know you are inside my fiber and heart

You are the sacred shadows in my blood

But I know I will return to you

So that my new light may reach you

My heart, which I have loved all along.

I adapted to specific personalities and environments and when I found the correct support, I knew the joke was up: my masks had to fall and my personality had to be re-formed back to another sense of self which was manageable for me. I had to learn how to meet the uncertainties I saw in the world, or else I'd never survive. Later in my healing, I learned of Internal Family Systems to help my whole self, which further deepened my healing journey.

I needed to cultivate anew the desire to live and a willingness to investigate who I really was. This was foreign to me. I had once believed I didn't have the skills to ground myself, or bring myself into a place of safety and healthy attachment. Seeking safety moment by moment was the only way I could manage.

Sometimes I would get sad and frustrated that I had to put so much effort into seeking safety for myself when it appeared others around me seemed to go about their daily business without much effort.

I needed to find a way in life and interactions with others where I felt in control and this practice was grounding for me.

Having a sense of safety and control minimized my anxiety. This all happened through trial and error, and I learned new tools like breathing, sharing honestly, and journaling in order to ground myself and recognize when I was going too far into feeling disconnected, or going to deep into worrying about uncertainty. Sometimes I would carry a small stone and hold it, or wear an elastic band on my wrist and flick it to snap out of a negative thought, and then I would focus on my breathing. I would also distract myself with music and day dreaming, and use my imagination in a healthy way. And, of course, participating in the natural world was my ultimate method of becoming grounded.

I began to see I no longer had to manipulate others and my environment in order to feel safe. Looking back I can see how I played the victim in many ways when I interacted with others, I can't think of a particular person I behaved this way to, but I do know in general I carried this victim presence.

Later, in psychology terms, I think it was sort of a learned helplessness in my personality. I felt in some sad way that I was the only person that endured the stresses of the world and even blamed the world for my problems.

In some ways I wanted to make people believe the world was out to get me, but this was only rationalizing poor behaviours or again my inability to form healthy connections.

Once I saw that people could see through my bullshit the game was over. I started to see that the world can actually be a safe place for me, where I can be vulnerable. The healthy, ideal life I try to achieve lies in realizing each day how essential it is for me to rest in emptiness. It was a relief to realize that it actually didn't take much effort to seek for places of safety in people and the world. I just needed the focus and determination to get there.

Coping with the World

Before that I often believed it was my job to make others believe I was coping with the world. Or that what others wanted was really important to me, and what a crock of shit that was. I know now that it's human nature to value what other people think of us, but it's unhealthy to take it to the point where we are consumed by or obsessed with the need for approval.

I often saw how I would start to play a victim role in certain situations, and when others said something to me like "you're okay," or "I'm sorry this happened," I felt, "I've got them now." Yet it was not at all proper to form a connection based on my insecure need to be rescued.

In addition I thought that this "victim" part of me would be able to evade responsibility for my actions, even when I harmed others. But I knew I was wearing a bullshit mask. I think now that my growth has happened more when people have confronted me in constructive ways about my behaviour. It hurts at first, but most people are very accurate. Even though I have gone through many things, this doesn't give me a ticket to ride. I have had to deal with setbacks and pains that all of us work through, and I'm not special. I don't get any privileges. This in many ways was a hard truth to embrace: the world doesn't owe me, and yes it's shitty.

I often felt I didn't have the ability to identify and communicate my emotions, and still today I dance around in my randomness of words on the edge of my dreams and visions. I know my thought process is different. But I embrace this.

The frustration for me was often the high expectation I had of others to understand me and automatically pick up on my signals, to know what and how I was communicating.

As I mentioned earlier in the memoir, I am and always have been a highly sensitive person.

Many people were challenged by my communication style. Some people would also tell me my style of communication was very random, nonsensical even, and they would tell me to hurry up with my story.

When others were impatient with me, I automatically felt they didn't want to hear what I had to say.

In college and university I learned to communicate more effectively through clinical supervision and constructive feedback. And I learned to be easy on myself as I realized that my feelings around my attempts to communicate were driven by an underlying anxiety and hyper-vigilance.

Sometimes when I was talking I could clearly see social cues that the words I was saying were not landing, and others weren't understanding what I was trying to communicate.

People would pause and maybe ask again what I was trying to get at. I also found I often needed to over share until I saw cues I was being understood, yet people would lose interest in my communication.

People also told me I pontificated and "jabbered on." I knew I was a poor communicator and I felt ashamed of this. Not once did I reflect upon how essential my communication style was to the development of intimacy.

I learned through deepening my spiritual understanding that most of my life I had been distracted by the "wrong" details and I often became hung up on my own reactions to them.

Today, I realize that part of building intimacy is about learning how to build a bridge to others. And I do this by simply listening.

Building Healthy Relationships

Throughout my early life, my connections with others remained tentative, and were limited to close relatives and friends, and acquaintances. I often felt there was no real chance for me to develop intimacy.

In my rougher days, I needed to know that other people knew what I needed for safety.

I suppose I didn't have the tools to cultivate real life connections until around age 20, which is a little late on the emotional scale. I

had to rely completely on some type of faith in myself and the belief I could slowly bring myself up to speed, slowly build and foster new relationships in a healthy giving and receiving way.

I had to realize that this process was being governed by what I felt were spiritual laws.

Currently, I am learning and growing into the idea and experience of what I feel is most essential in terms of intimacy. That is vulnerability or the need to be vulnerable.

Sometimes I felt ashamed that when others provided care and security and communication to me, I could not receive it, yet there often was in that moment some form of soul connection that was cultivating a learning experience for me that was somehow beyond my awareness.

Even now, when family and friends tell me authentically that they love me, I still may struggle with it.

I have learned to give of my time and experiences through my career as a helping professional, and have recognized that it's easier to love in that context because boundaries are already established through laws and regulations.

Another aspect of disillusionment for me was the constant thought that if I were to develop healthy connections, how would I handle the failure of those connections?

I had no skills for endings and closures, which I have since learned is a common experience for trauma survivors.

I would feel in many ways that I was being abandoned or I was doing the abandonment if I decided to end my connections. There was also this fear of losing the protective connection I had felt to Nature.

Yet now I know that building authentic connections with others will only add to the full sphere of my life. I never once thought I could have my connection to Nature and people in one full circle. I had to work at creating the space for both. I suppose the opposite of disillusionment is the idea of embracing all areas to connect with life.

One thing I have noticed as I've grown healthy is that I now know I have choices about who I want to be and how I want to relate to others, and how much energy I want to invest in other people.

I used to think connecting with people may have been at the root of my problems, but I eventually came to see it was really more about *who* I was connecting with, and for which reasons, that had been messing me up.

Now I know I can determine what level of intimacy I will allow with people, and this helps me think about how much I can offer, without guilt or fear. My inner critic used to always tell me I'd given all I could give (in terms of love), but I now know that's bullshit. I've given of myself, but it was all the wrong things and with all the wrong people.

The more healthy I became, the more I saw I was able to give to people who really meant something to me, and who were also able and healthy enough themselves to receive it.

In real life interactions, we all have to work at boundaries and develop our own laws and communicate honestly, which is work. Part of me is like, screw this shit, why should I have to work at this? It's just more difficult for me because of my sensitivity.

Yet now, currently, I realize I am becoming more civilized and I am in the same boat as everyone else. We all have to learn how to bring the right amount of time and space into our close relationships. I can now appreciate the efforts people put into caring and that makes me want to invest in my relationships with them as well. We are rewarded for our good behaviours by having an opportunity to be kind to others. This is the healthiness of being selfless and giving without manipulating others, giving with no other reward than the chance to be more helpful.

Wow, for a person who was so self-absorbed this was a bloody Christmas miracle! With continued health, I am also learning to see where others tried to provide security and caring for me in my past and I've come to value the efforts family and friends have made to do that.

Furthermore, when I was getting out of my own self-pity and loathing and creating my own despair, I began to see where others were really suffering from despair and difficulties themselves. Although I was able to form my own refuge in my meditative meadow, I started to see others wandering the way I had.

Accepting Love

It confused me at times because people saw me as vibrant and gentle and approachable—they would say I was quiet and always reflective.

Often, however, on the inside I was hurting and scared. I later learned this was another true hallmark of being a survivor of abuse, and having little confidence. My acceptance of this new power of love that I was experiencing more and more each day helped me beyond words.

I recall when I began early recovery from alcohol, mental health issues, and trauma, some people told me I would experience a life beyond my wildest dreams, and they were accurate. One phrase I heard once that has always stayed with me was: "People will love you until you are able to love yourself." I would also add that people would still continue to love me and care for me.

As you're reading this, I invite you to reflect on the love people felt for you at times when it was difficult for you to love yourself. The 12-Step fellowship, many family members and friends, and my therapist helped move this process along for me. In particular I had a good friend tell me one day that I was showing signs of being confident. And this helped me to see that my inside self was matching my outside behaviours

Practicing self-confidence was not easy and it required me to jump into new experiences and take risks. I said "yes" to that date, enrolled in a course at university, embraced an attitude of trying the things that came along, and dealt with the outcome, whatever it was. I accepted each experience and believed I had the tools to deal with whatever the outcome would be.

So, in each moment of interaction, I mentally and sometimes gently forced myself to feel those vulnerabilities and listen to my own gut. I practiced saying kind words in my mind, such as "May I accept my vulnerabilities," and "May I be free from any fears."

Over time, connections formed and I realized my brain was also learning new skills: my anxiety lessened. And by having more confidence, I started to see I have choices as to what interactions would be healthy for me.

Intimacy can still be a struggle for me and I still find myself going back to that same territory, trying to contemplate a new area in my vision of the meadow where I can nurture and cultivate this aspect of my life.

I can no longer rely on my mind to figure things out around my fears of closeness and intimacy.

I can often find myself getting enmeshed in the emotions of others, and I start thinking about their behaviours—and how I am affecting their behaviour—so much so, in fact, that I stop being aware of how my own behaviour is unfolding or how it affects others. And, if my behaviours are not well-received by others when closeness is occurring, I freeze or run. This creates feelings of shame. Again, I am learning that this happens with other people, too.

Now during this process of growing as an intimate man, I find I get confused. I wonder if I'm being genuine when I share my pain, and I wonder what my motive is. Or am I just looking for attention?

I am learning that I need to ensure I have the time I need to process these issues. I need to go to that meadow and reflect and sit with the feelings, and examine them without fear.

It took me a long time to see the value of people. I had to learn to see beyond the fears that people had, and the cruelty that sometimes exists within them, too. Somebody once said to me that pain will make people do crazy things.

I think of so many people now, as I write this memoir, who have crossed my path and have taught me love and light. My aunts Christine and Kathleen and Ellen. All my uncles and family in Alberta. My mother and father and, of course, my wonderful stepmother, Janet Lyttle.

In fact, there are so many friends and acquaintances that deserve mention that I would have to write another book focusing on the gifts they bring in order to do them all justice. Which is not how I used to feel.

In my past I only sought out relationships I knew would require little-to-no effort to cultivate. I believe this was because I did not want to have that responsibility, and I was lazy. I also believed I did not deserve true, authentic connections with others.

I often blamed others when things went sour so I didn't have to be responsible for breakdowns in my relationships.

Ultimately, as I grew healthier in my understanding of the natural, normal way society works, I became attracted to other healthy folks with whom I could learn new social skills that were important for my survival.

I had to learn a new sense of responsibility in my relationships, although some may still argue that in my attempts at becoming healthy, I ended up rupturing some potential relationships. At the same time, I realize I must have seen something unhealthy in these people that didn't sit right with me. I believe I was learning from my errors.

I could start to see how much responsibility and energy I was able to invest in situations and in my relationships. I had to experience rejection, as well, and perhaps abandonment, and I had to learn how to respond to them in healthy ways. And this is where my developing self-compassion skills helped.

The love that I now have the capacity to provide is simply an expression of gratitude to life and all the people who were instrumental to my growth through childhood and recovery.

I can reflect now upon how uncomfortable I often felt when other people said I was loved, and now I can accept that people can love me, with all my faults. When people say, "I love you," or, "we care about you," or, "you mean the world to me," I now take it all in, rather than turn the words into self-hatred.

I used to say that in early recovery people loved me until I was able to love myself. I was always frightened that I might actually be able to love – and I know I can indeed love. But now I am learning to have no shame in seeking closeness with others, I am not special because I may have intimacy issues: we all do. As a good friend of mine once said to me, we are human, we will hurt others again, and we will get hurt.

I see now that the real breakthroughs come when we look honestly at our motives and take responsibility for our actions. To me this doesn't mean a simple apology; it requires the hard task of being willing to change a behaviour.

I believe I—along with the rest of the human race—will most likely have this challenge until I die. I can now see that moments of discomfort in a relationship are opportunities for more growth and awareness.

They are opportunities for me to provide myself with love and compassion and also to provide love, forgiveness and compassion to others.

This awareness now motivates me to take even more risks in bonding with new people all the time. Where I was once a pretender, I am now just another guy seeking healthy connections with others.

Selfishness and trying to navigate through pain do not leave room for self–love and forgiveness. Most importantly, I now try not to fall into the old victimization template I developed early on in my life. This process always set me up for more self-pity and loathing in fear and shame.

Another essential area of growth lay in my perception of intimacy in the realm of sexuality. Being healthy has enabled me to strive for a more healthy understanding of sexuality and my masculinity.

I now have a level of self-compassion that allows me to fully understand the needs of my body and I can work towards having the freedom to explore, and see the meaning behind life's other pleasures.

Practicing mindful self-compassion has taught me to notice and embrace all of the sensations in my body, and it has expanded my capacity to examine my thoughts.

6   The Good Suffering

Although I was getting healthier and feeling more grounded, I knew deep inside there were still many things I struggled with.

For example: I still felt at times an anxiety around people. I get anxious just thinking about it, which I believe stems from the fact that some parts of my brain are hard wired to be hyper-vigilant, and I am sensitive to the behaviour of other people. I really need to see if there is potential for harm.

Yet, I have since learned in recovery recently that I have to try and work around this inner hyper-vigilance, or else I may never fully form better connections. I guess I've had to accept there might be in life times when I will get hurt. There are times when relatives and even good friends have harmed me with things they have done or said, but I've had to be resilient around that. I've had to start stepping into connections where I might end up hearing things I didn't want to hear.

However, I've also had to start enjoying life, too—I don't think Life was meant to consist solely of this constant searching of self and self-discovery that I've become so adept at.

At one point I struggled with a particular job I held. There was a conflict between my values and the role I was hired to play. I was, at times, exhausted from compromising.

Typically I discovered through my work life that I really sucked at interpersonal skills and understanding social cues and although I could engage easily in dialogue, internally I would still be saying negative things to myself.

For example some very common thoughts were: "you will never learn how to connect with others in the work world," and, "you don't have what it takes to truly hold down a consistent job," and, "why do you always search for blame and create conflict?"

In this particular job, things started to get to me and I had serious conflict brewing with my direct supervisor. Finally in a meeting one afternoon, she said, " you know, maybe this isn't the job for you." At first I found it hard to accept, but deep inside I knew she was right.

Many times my own troubles are from my own making. I always felt I should fight for what I believed was right. I know it is very common with survivors to have difficulty with people in authority positions and the same patterns tend to repeat.

In life, as we know, we will get knocked down, and people will be assholes; we will have very poor managers and co-workers, and sometimes, family members, too. I remember one of my sponsors in AA tell me once that sometimes we learn more from the negative people in our life than the perceptively positive people because they force us to look at some things differently.

When I started to value tough times as being great learning opportunities, I began to really feel like I was living. I stopped fighting or avoiding my fears and I embraced the idea that I was not meant to suffer.

Trauma and the Brain

In my trauma recovery now, I am also very aware of daily triggers and I am trying to learn how to embrace them to see what they can teach me.

Physiologically, I believe the brain is an amazing organ that can heal trauma in time and I like to believe that any experience I have had since I've been willing to look into my psyche, is only there for the good of my health.

Experiencing painful memories—and even re-traumatizing my brain—now only allows my brain to build up new muscle and strength, perhaps even build the type of resilience and strength I should have had when I was age seven.

For example, I recall waking up from a dream in a panic. The dream had replayed the real memory of a time when I was around age six or seven—not too long after I had been abused—when every night for three nights I urinated in a small plastic McDonald's gift bag and then placed the bag under my bed. I think each bag was actually a puppet with all the McDonald's characters on it.

Each morning I felt a sense of intense shame and confusion, followed by some sadness and then, throughout the day, I carried this sadness with me, thinking of the little boy who had done this. Why would I behave this way? I was sick, I wasn't normal. I told myself all kinds of negative things about myself, which contributed to forming an idea of the person I thought I was.

But then, as I suffered through this dream aftermath and memory, I gave myself credit. I was behaving in a way that perhaps indicated I was protecting myself from something, as I now suspect, and this insight is due to the training into behaviour and mental health I've acquired for the work I do today.

Another "good " aspect of suffering is that it brings us closer to a common shared human experience. We all suffer in various degrees.

So how do we mend ourselves? Well, I bring myself back to my early AA teachings: I am no longer alone. This was one of the major teachings from my self –compassionate learning: we all share the commonality of our suffering. This made sense to me when I look back at my early AA life.

The common bond shared with other people in recovery was that we had all been through very dark and devastating times with alcoholism.

Many nights when I went to AA meetings in the Hamilton area I saw the slogan on the wall "You are Not Alone." Reading this simple phrase brought me a great sense of freedom at the time, and it still does.

Another positive aspect of contemplating very difficult emotions is the opportunity to detach from pathologizing and analyzing every single event or experience we've had.

I first started to change this thinking when a friend told me I needed to stop searching for a solution for things and hold on to my questions. I didn't like this at all. As a matter of fact I was angry and depressed for days after our conversation. But he was right. My inquiring mind can get the best of me and it's a hindrance to my growth. I needed to see how silence and quiet contemplation could become an internal tool which could help me know my limitations, watch my expectations, and help me connect with others.

Authentic Connections

Through the tough work of digging away at recovery and healing I began to realize there were many times in my youth when I did feel authentic connections with people. This is the kind of light I hope my story will shine for people.

It is tough, no doubt, but if you are a survivor of childhood trauma, mental health challenges, and/or addiction issues, there can be light and freedom at the end of the hard work. The true gift of working hard and letting go of pain has been that I was finally able to begin to see the power of goodness in my life.

For example, I remember soft ball games with the Nahawkahides in Heinsburg Park, Alberta, visits to the Calaway Park Amusement Centre in Alberta, and time spent at the Calgary Zoo.

It is difficult to avoid here at this point the cliché of "Time Heals," yet there are so many truths to this statement. Fifteen years of sobriety have taught me new ideas about life and new ways for me to broaden my faith. And as my mind cleared, I began to see it was necessary to have more action in my life. Although some relationships and other aspects of my life generated what seemed like major failures, I was learning to say, as my good friend Brad Henderson shared with me once, "I tried."

Wounded Healer / Lee Lyttle

In time, I became adept at entering the meadow and walking down that beautiful and difficult path of self-discovery, but it took quite a while before I became purely motivated to change things I might be struggling with. It required self-compassion with a dedication to being who I am in all areas of my life, to accept my thoughts and actions as being exactly as they were meant to be, without harm, of course, to others or myself.

Although I had experienced a trauma related to the assault I had experienced, I had to learn to suffer differently if I were to survive in the way all human beings do. This was "a good suffering" that I wanted to access.

Suffering is a tool to break down and teach ourselves what we value and what we need. In my view, we've lost a sense of the relationship between suffering and contentment. Happiness is a man-made state of suffering, in a way, and I believe striving after the idea of being in a permanent state of happiness is a delusion.

Earlier on in my life I, like everyone, strived to achieve this ideal. and it ultimately became painful when the reality set in that nothing constructed from society helps you fulfill this idea.

My true contentment came from keeping close to the reality that there is almost nothing in my external world that can make me happy. All my contentment and fleeting states of joy or happiness are born through my internal reality of suffering, connection, faith and contemplation of my spiritual self.

We are taught to fear the task of working away at this true state of contentment because it involves looking at aspects of ourselves and life which are undesirable.

I invite readers to ask what your own suffering may be teaching you? Do you hang on to suffering in an attempt to control your life? Does it shape you and teach you how to be hungry for more vulnerability, whether you experience trauma or not?

Humanity shares the common bond of suffering and shame. My own experiences of suffering can show up in many forms and, again, they are typically prompted by relational or interpersonal difficulties.

125

Acknowledging I am suffering in some way is a first step towards resolving it. There is a saying that helps me do this: "Name it, Claim it, Tame it."

Another tool is the practice of recognizing that something somebody has said or done can be viewed positively as an opportunity for growth and learning. That is not to say I seek out interpersonal problems to help me develop; we all know the world has no shortage of circumstances we can stumble over each day without going looking for new ones.

Equally true is the fact that there are millions of self-help methods and memes available—including humour, which in many ways is an advanced defense mechanism. We see this prevalent in social media, specifically. I know I have to admit that the amount of time I spend on social media is unhealthily high at times, which means that I may be causing myself unnecessary suffering. And I feel we each have a responsibility to examine the things in our lives—our habits, and patterns—which may cause unnecessary pain or even simply teach us something about ourselves.

Grounded Contemplation

I have experienced many incidents that changed my perspective of suffering from something to fear to something that can bring me directly into moments of grounded contemplation.

I've felt the pure shock of an inner shift, which leaves me with yet more inner awareness of my relationship with a power or creator greater than myself. The experience has entailed obedience, discipline, and care.

I have also trusted that the right people will cross my path to teach me what I need to know next.

At times this has happened while I was in a heavy depression, fighting against despair, when someone, even a stranger, would say something to me. The words would sink in, as though my ears cleared enough to take them in.

This contrasts with what I consider my "poor" suffering, which happened when I sought to hear the things I wanted to hear, and not what I needed to hear, or what God felt my entire self needed to absorb.

`Looking back, I realize the most valuable things I ended up truly hearing or experiencing during my path to wellness required me to do little more than say "yes," show up, and bring my body: I've been on thousands of fishing trips, and vacations, and there was a period of time when my old friend and sponsor, Bill D., would have me travel with his family and my other AA fellowship members to southern Pennsylvania in the summer to go white water rafting. I was grateful to have the opportunity to grow and be with healthy people.

Bill D. was a powerful example of action to me. I believe he demonstrated many of the attitudes in life I was seeking to emulate. But he also showed his humanity and frailty. These experiences gave me a good suffering or what some call "growing pains," because I was making a choice to put myself into new life experiences. I was excited and happy overall, yet inside I had to chip away at my insecurities.

In some cases, I recall holding my feelings in check and saving all my terror until I was alone, when I could give myself permission to shake and cry. Each time this happened, I had to work through the pain, and it was purposeful, because it meant I was growing and changing.

Now I have confidence in myself and I am comfortable being myself while in social situations, and I am comfortable thereafter. And I am aware of my growth. As adults I don't think we share our experiences around continuing to grow up quite often enough.

When I talk with another adult my age, or even older, and they say they are still learning, there is a little light that starts beaming in me. It flickers boldly when they admit that we are all still seeking meaning, and that no one has really figured it all out yet. Although some people pretend to know how to live life, it's really bullshit.

There were also times when I felt unsettled immediately after somebody said something to me I didn't like. This was because their comment carried within it a truth, or a version of reality. In a way, I felt that God had sent these moments to me to show me I could no longer manipulate people or situations to create a more preferable outcome for me, usually one where I felt in control. However from a behavioural perspective, having a sense of control was actually very poor for my health, and it caused more severe consequences, one of which was feeling spiritually lost and experiencing a crisis of faith.

I heard somebody say once that they always struggled with loneliness. This was their greatest war, and I believe this has been true for me, too. Because of the loneliness I struggled with, I always needed attention. In fact I craved it. But perhaps I was suffering in the wrong ways.

The problem was that I didn't have the skills to allow myself to be vulnerable and, in turn, allow myself to seek real, genuine ways to receive attention from others. I know this is a human need; it's how we develop a social network. And, in turn, how we build our safety net, so that when we fall, we have safety.

I always truly wanted to get the right attention. However, I only sought attention where I could continue to hide my pain and the fact that I was hurting. I often wrestled with the Universe around this issue, mostly because I believe the Universe wants to wrestle with us, and will not let go of us easily. We have a relationship with it, whether we like it or not. We may hide in our culture, which is often full of addictions. But the Universe always knows where to find us.

Over time I became aware that most of my problems stemmed from core beliefs of being unlovable. What is the antidote? Many things come to mind, but the first part of the journey began in July of 2015 when I experienced repeated thoughts of self–forgiveness during a road trip across Canada and the United States. I knew ahead of time that this trip was going to involve a search for self-forgiveness. I knew it was going to be difficult work.

Wounded Healer / Lee Lyttle

As I drove into the prairies I began to think. There was something fundamental here that was setting me on fire with a new energy for life. I refer to my little silver Honda Civic as my chapel, my sanctuary, and my church. The confession booth is built within the dash and when the rubber hits the highway, a frequency of prayer and reflection resonates within me.

What people normally refer to as a "Road Trip" I see as a pilgrimage, a time to sort things out. My playlist was ready, and loaded with Jewel, Neil Young, The Smiths, the Everly Brothers, Buddy Hollie, and an audio book: *Of Mice and Men* by John Steinbeck.

I surrendered to the highway on that trip and after I pitched my tent in a field along the way, I saw my body alight and walking close to the grassy shores of the field beside the road; the light from the dark open skies fell onto the wheat making it look like the sea.

I stood on a slope and turned to face the hills, then turned again to walk back to my tent. I saw myself again detached. I am my soul walking on the road. I felt my sadness and loss and took responsibility for the mistakes I had made, yet I also took responsibility for moving forward.

I know that wounding myself was not necessary. I think true growth requires a person to really accept their imperfections, mistakes, and failures.

I used to ask myself, "Why am I suffering fears, self-delusion?" People would say to me that the multiverse had forgiven me, yet I did not agree. I could not see any signs that this was true. I felt deeply hurt, and I knew the thoughts I was having.

But my soul cannot dwell on what is done. I had to harvest this, and "clean my house," as they say. Work at it, get it done! I have learned to work away at a living amends process by giving back to life and by giving to—and helping—those I see in need. The great crisis I have created for myself lay in not sharing my crisis with those who might find comfort through it.

A Path to Forgiveness

Forgiveness is about accepting responsibility for our actions. But not dwelling on them all.

Shame is the evil which kept me pinned to my own madness. I had to believe and accept in my heart that God does not see me as incapable of receiving forgiveness. And, in fact, that this may be the only forgiveness that is important. Morbid reflection, distractions, getting trapped in my emotions…they are all manifestations of my shame.

I used to think that when people said I was emotionally healthy, and had emotional intelligence, that this was the ticket for me to be accepted by others. But deep inside, it was difficult for me to forgive myself when I felt deep shame for feeling like I did not live up to my own ideal, or the ideals that people placed upon me.

At this point in my experience I was awakening to new visions of myself, learning what my visions meant to me, learning and accepting that I am the sum of my visions, how I rest, and how I seek.

When I work through my many notes from that trip, I see how I once again examined my identity in terms of my ideas and concepts related to spirituality.

People from time to time will be curious about what lies below the surface of me.

And I look to my heart's language for moral teachings and I have come to realize that morals and government and Identity, laws and justice, are found in the dirt and sky and water—and all the life—in the forest. This is my language, and perhaps it is why I am drawn to cultures that value these aspects of our world as well.

I struggle with my non-conformist attitude and it causes many conflicts for me. It also causes me feelings of disconnection.

When I feel like the conflicts are close to causing me major difficulties, I seek for the basics again in food, warmth and rest.

Wounded Healer / Lee Lyttle

I have found that when I am detached I am sensitive to negativity around me and I remember my HALT strategy: am I Hungry, Angry, Lonely or Tired? It's getting easier for me to remember that a challenge in any one of these areas affects the others, and they increase the likelihood I will act out in destructive ways. I think of the opposite of HALT: Full, Peaceful, Connected, and Rested. There is no acronym for this but the words are nice just the way they are.

One area I visited on that trip out West was the Crow Agency Pow Wow in Montana. During my stay at the Pow Wow, I had moments of deep despair related to the ending of my marriage and I hated myself. I was led to a couple of booths and tents on the grounds where there were Christian counsellors who assisted me with deep examination of self-forgiveness and ultimately myself. Following this amazing solo trip I felt a new sense that I was able to grow through this difficult life change without running away and destroying myself.

Through more tears and gut-wrenching emotions, I had to communicate with God like I never had before. I was learning that, although I believed God had forgiven me, I continued to persecute myself, harm myself.

A deep hatred for myself grew stronger as I tapped into the flowing spring of deep beliefs about my defective, unlovable self.

Now it was time to reach my core as I knew this was a critical point in my life where I had to either decide I was going to fade back into a deeper despair that could possibly bring me to a point where either the bottle would claim me, or death would.

But the phrase "willingness to go to any length" in my journey and recovery was deeply ingrained into my psyche. All those recovery meetings I had attended worked. I had never seen how much I hated myself, I had been causing myself more trauma by trying not to accept things as they were, I could no longer get caught up in denial. This is perhaps the vulnerable part of me: I had to believe that God had only seen the best part of me, where I only saw the worst, and I felt I wasn't the only one who saw my darkness. I had asked God, "What part of me is avoiding and keeping me separated from You?" This was also my authentic self, asking me what I needed to do now, what actions could I take to find peace again? I believed this creative force saw every fibre of my being.

My objective was to try to gain an understanding of what God-Consciousness meant to me, to see what God's perspective was on everything. This was essential for me to gain a healthy perspective of the new change in my life, another experience of deep loss. It was important for me to realize that my thinking was moral and right under these circumstances.

It was a big task to look at my past, but not to linger there and morbidly reflect on what had happened. We all do this, look into the past and ask, "What was the meaning behind this event, why did I have to experience this? Why did I struggle through so many phases in my life when others seemed to flow through them with grace and acceptance?"

I thought I was trying to be an example of His will in my relationships, through my actions to help others, but in true spiritual learning this thought was highly inaccurate because it placed me into a position where I felt I knew what was good for people.

I saw that I had more impact when I showed others that I struggled but ultimately reached peace and contentment through my struggles, than when I believed I knew what God's will was.

In the deepening awareness of my recovery, I could now see where I had been making unhealthy choices my whole life; I had been working hard to mask my behaviour and avoid accepting my imperfections and severe low self-confidence. I continue to attend regular AA meetings now, but in the form of on-line groups due to my remote location.

I now feel able in many ways to practice what I have learned in real life. Recovery in the beginning involved, of course, brutal and painful work. Recovery in trauma and addictions, I have had to accept, will be a life-long endeavor. I am okay with that.

I choose to still understand myself through my recovery lens and embrace all human qualities in my daily life. I feel that consistent, dedicated attendance at AA meetings earlier on built a foundation of safety that helps me know that if I really need to get more support I can easily tap back into it. For example, if I notice I am isolating, or cancelling social events too many times, I might be getting into trouble.

I depend upon the direct counsel of my friends. Some people refer to their initial recovery path as being like being parented. And as in any parent–child relationship, there comes a time for more autonomy. As I may have mentioned, fortunately, with my newfound autonomy, I searched for other methods to get what we call "outside help" in AA. I sought out various therapists to help me work through problems relating to relationships, trauma, sexual issues, male issues, family, connections, and anxiety.

In addition, I knew that at some point I needed to dig deep into how my sexual trauma was related to my addiction to alcohol. Quite simply it was another way to cope with pain and avoid and deny how broken I felt I was. Secretly in my mind, I remember saying to myself, *tonight I will drink so much alcohol that my goal will be not to wake up in the morning.*

Seeking Support

I most likely could write a whole chapter on my therapy journey and the outside help I received. There is no shame in seeking more support. Clearly I knew I how damaged I felt I was, therefore, I knew I needed to keep up rigorous efforts to learn new coping skills and find sanity. Especially in my ever-changing world.

I have seen many people come and go. Some friends could not find peace, and this hurts. When people ask me about my view on addictions, sometimes I feel I really have nothing to say. I believe each person has his or her own spiritual journey to sort out. Ultimately, we all may need to come to terms with how we avoid or get trapped in denial regarding our own human experience. Sometimes I think we throw the word "addiction" around too freely, along with what we consider our knowledge about what that actually is.

Some people believe there is no evidence we can be addicted to things. I believe our brain is complex and our behaviour is really driven by many aspects of it.

I believe each individual's brain is built through thousands of environmental, biological, physiological, emotional, spiritual, and cognitive pathways. One area of that is, of course, related to pleasure. I believe this human experience is all about learning to both suffer and have sanity.

We shouldn't be surprised if we get sick, because we have failed to accept the fullness of our human experience. So we do things that trigger the pleasure part of our brain, our amygdala. Again, bear with me as I am only sharing from experience, but this I believe is the area that needs to be regulated. It deals with our chemicals (the release of Dopamine).

Somehow we have found behaviours and substances that increase the flow of this chemical and sometimes it's very shitty when we may have failed to regulate our thoughts and emotions to the reality of our environment.

We are in constant pursuit of avoiding pain, disconnect, and discomfort. It makes sense. But in my learning it's not realistic. It states in the book, *The 12 Steps and 12 Traditions* that no one really wants to do good things, nobody really wants to be honest all the time. Yet if we need to do these things to survive, we work at regulation.

We work at allowing our brains to do what it naturally needs to do. And what is that, you may ask? Well that, to me, is a mystery. I believe the pain we experience is the profound disconnect we actually feel when we become aware of how sick we may be, spiritually, emotionally, or cognitively.

Sometimes, we may find we can switch addictions or unhealthy attachments. One thing I have noticed in the past few years is an overwhelming societal desire to tap into yoga, Eastern philosophy, and meditation, along with an obsession with creating intriguing motivational quotes and creating an environment in one's home that would give Martha Stewart a nervous breakdown.

We have an ability to create a peaceful environment, and trust me, I love nice things. Yet, this also could be avoidance or as another term I've learned fashions it, a "spiritual bypass"—the idea that you can reach enlightenment by doing little, if any, of the work necessary to get there. To me, in some ways this behaviour is disrespectful to those survivors who are actually trying to find sanity and peace. Having a sense of your own Beauty and purpose in the world, in my view, should only be an addition to the very hard internal work that a person has accomplished. I suppose we as a culture are still determined to get the "quick fix" of experiencing joy and abundance without doing the hard work. This often proves to be fatal.

Beautiful Things

Beautiful things, in my view, should only be additional to the very hard internal work a person undertakes. We are all too prone to deny the truth about ourselves. Or in other words, we delude ourselves and often have an inability to see ourselves for who we really are.

Many years of therapy helped me realize I needed to become more honest about how I am in the current moment if I wanted to survive.

I had a breakthrough once when I walked into an AA meeting and another member simply asked, "how are you? as we all typically do. And I was honest and said, "I'm a little fucked up right now." Simply saying that out loud brought so much relief.

In my opinion, I believe we avoid being truthful about how we are because we recognize at some level that once we expose who we really are, we have opened ourselves up to being responsible and accountable for our thoughts and actions. Because now somebody has seen the truth about us. But if this is a process of love and care, then our efforts to become responsible may not be as difficult a task as we make it out to be. I take comfort now in my imperfections and the silly failures that happen to me.

Regarding recovery in trauma and addictions, I am okay with the fact that this will be a life-long endeavor.

I choose to work to understand myself through my recovery lens and I embrace all human qualities in my daily life. I find my brain actually has started to do what it's naturally supposed to do.

And regarding awareness of suffering and pain, I can regulate in some way through connection to healthy things, trying to eat right and undertaking some physical exercise, although I really hate the gym. I get outside a lot instead.

In my spiritual growth I have been fortunate to continue to have a willingness to grow.

This willingness has helped me understand how action is important in my life, simply because I am an over-thinker. I will naturally attempt to sort things out intellectually, which is, and has been, very problematic.

My fears have all subsided when I have been honest with others and vulnerable in the fellowship of the human race.

Now I am discovering the real natural process of this human experience, everything in all its glory, even the pain and suffering, and I am learning how to still use that creative imagination and visualize the meadow, the bridges, and the natural world to help keep me grounded.

Learning to keep the grounding of my imagination where it belongs, on the ground. Learning to see my mind and thinking as also a tool, to contemplate, wonder, have curiosity and imagine.

But to also know how to not overthink and stay stuck in my mind. I have to admit that I will still get triggered and experience states like conflict, indecision, and lack of acceptance.

We tend to pathologize and diagnose every single little frailty we have now in our world, and it does bother me. I think we need to get back to the experience that what you may be feeling is actually normal considering what you may be going through.

136

Wounded Healer / Lee Lyttle

I see trauma conferences everywhere and new and bold psychologies about the brain and trauma crop up regularly, which is all amazing, don't get me wrong... but I get upset when I see some parts of our culture exploit this.

I read recently somewhere that those with real mental health concerns in Toronto were upset because there seemed to be a growing sub-culture of those who exploit or romanticize mental illness as if it's glamorous to have a low mood or " be dark."

Suffering and pain have become catalysts for change for me. In AA there is a saying: "Pain is the touchstone of all spiritual progress."

My father's passing brought me a whole space of new emotions and thoughts I had never previously encountered. At times, like most, I ventured into heavy confusion and terror.

I felt a complete loss of control and an overwhelming emptiness. I tried to figure out where my father was now—in the shed? In the kitchen cooking poor man's Irish stew? Hooking up the trailer for the ATV? Or napping while watching old John Wayne Westerns?

I also had feelings of guilt that I should've cried more than I did, until a good friend of mine told me that's normal and that I had been moving through the grieving process well because I knew in my heart my father loved me and I believed he knew I loved him. I have to believe that I care when I say I do.

In our trauma therapy, and in our culture of addictions and even the research we do into addictions, we tend to focus on only certain aspects of trauma. But we are gaining new levels of understanding each day.

And I think many trauma survivors would agree that triggers can have a positive impact on helping us see exactly what an issue is truly about. It serves a purpose, however painful; and this could be one of the greatest assets in trauma recovery that we have.

I see the benefits of a good suffering in my willingness today to seek guidance in calling myself to truth in all my errors or defects. These moments are often triggered by a social event or interaction. I could see when I attempted to manipulate others so I could escape and run from an intolerable situation. Once I was aware of this, I had to challenge myself to stay in that difficulty. I did this only through God's grace.

One important aspect of suffering lies in learning how to hold moments of pain as a tool to further reflect with God. And learn how to embrace the uncertainty of things. And to learn to love mystery. Deeper meanings to questions will be revealed in their proper time.

In contemplation I have often thought of the phrase "be still and know that I am God." To be brought to a place of peace and silence is the ultimate gift of pain. When I become aware that I am isolating myself from love, I can also experience shame that I would run from love, true love.

But God has been so faithful to me. No matter how much I run, I keep coming back to the ultimate power of His grace.

Although I have had to learn the pains of naturally being rejected from society, perhaps, or even rejected by others, nothing is more painful than being in isolation from God. Even the moments of deep despair and pity and sadness I've encountered in my life can't match the misery of feeling disconnected from God. In my belief, wallowing in self-pity or resentments may be a contributing factor to mental health.

By now, my meadow has grown all around me, I can see my path winding and turning into the shade of the shoreline willows, the sunlight flickering through the river. My heart beating to each flow of the water surfacing over the grasses. I place my emotions in my secret box, all good and bad and hold them there. I keep my box by the shore. Dragonflies rise up from the small marsh and fly past my shoulders. Bees settle on the daisy flowers and wild flowers.

7 Breaking Through: An Awakening

When I speak of spiritual matters, I refer to my higher power as God, Creative Intelligence, Creator, Engineer, or Soul. I've learned this works for me so I only ask that you embrace an open mind throughout this chapter and try not to let these terms distract you.

I use the term "awakening" seriously, and not in a new age-y spiritual way. True awakening for me is accepting many harsh realities about yourself and your beliefs. In addition, my idea of awakening is that it is experiential and on-going, a sort of progressive unfolding of truth.

When I look back now to times of change and transition I think again, "Man, what pulled me through?" This process of awakening was in fact a real farewell to darkness.

Prior to my awakening, I had increasing levels of clarity around the old self that was dying away. I sensed that I was a stranger in my own skin. Now that stranger has let go of his old world, and I never have to step foot in it again. I said goodbye. And in those moments of clarity, the whole world of humanity began to embrace me.

The person I had been at age 15, sitting on a kitchen floor with knife in hand, pointing the blade at my belly, sobbing, and wanting to die, was now a miracle.

What do we mean when we talk about miracles? Think of your own experiences where there was an incident of mystery in how things changed around you. My miracles started to occur when I felt inside that what I was actually doing was right.

Miracles are being able to see yourself smile and hear yourself laugh for the first time. To walk on the sunny side of the street. To feel yourself reach down on a path and press a yellow rose into your snout. Believing that you are finally beginning to feel connected and loved. A knowing that you may be even be able to love others, too.

I believe each of us has had experiences, call them what you like, that generated a major shift in perspective, sometimes without provocation. An experience perhaps we cannot and may never be able to explain.

I've learned from many people who've shared a wide variety of experiences in faith. Some I have questioned and I am thankful for their answers.

Once I had an individual give me my spirit name and all he did was look at my dragonfly tattoo and said, " your spirit name is Dragonfly and I was like, "Fuck, that's disappointing." But I believe keeping an open mind to others' faith-related explorations is the greatest way for me to practice my own idea of faith. To me my beliefs about who I am are always progressing and evolving.

Many people I have met have experienced change. Their eyes and behaviours, the way they talk, their actions—have all changed; you are witness to their expansion. Awakening to me is a progressive term. At 23 years sober, I am only beginning, at times, to see how I can change or have changed. Deep insights are always being revealed to me and I see my life unfolding each day.

I always thought I had a romance with change, with everything. But it was only romance I learned from the movies. There comes a time in everyone's healing journey when you have the realization that excavating your past simply becomes too exhausting, that sifting through unnecessary defects serves no purpose for you.

Part of the difficulty for me when I go down into my meditations and self-examination lies in seeing how quickly my mind can distort things, events, and people. I can quickly fall prey to despair and annihilation.

Now, the sign of real growth is my ability to restore my mind back into a state of peace. As we all know now, we are, it seems, in a period where we are sitting with more questions then perhaps ever before. There is no doubt that this book landed for you for some purpose.

I saw myself how my eyes slowly opened up to moments of clarity or experiences of a deeper truth about who we are and what our purpose is. Thankfully my editor kept me focused and grounded many times to push through and gain some conclusion with this project, and I know the healing and learning will continue in other capacities

The Awakening of Humanity

It is truly an amazing moment when you become aware that you are a part of the awakening of humanity.

Along my journey, I have met many amazing, wonderful and wise people who have taught me deep lessons about life and myself.

People have often appeared in my life at the perfect time. People seemed to show up precisely when I was about to fall into a pit of dark thoughts and they were there for me on my path when I came crawling out of the valley. I can be distant from everything in one breath and feel like I have the stars in my palm in another.

At times I sat on the park bench of humanity. Yet I was always pissed that I just sat along the sidelines of life when what I wanted was to jump into the action.

In reflection, there have been two major tools on my path as I walked closer to the meadow in my vision. The first tool is called Step 5, a gift from Alcoholics Anonymous that invites us to admit to the God of our concept and understanding, to ourselves, and to another human being, the exact nature or our wrongs.

The second tool is about developing my own inner voice to the point where I can finally trust to some degree its guidance. We may call it many things, but lately I simply borrow what most people may refer to as "your gut."

The more I developed good character from interacting with more positive healthy people doing healthy things, the more my own awakening deepened.

I became hungry for the aspects of humanity I saw were on the rise of goodness and love. This connection overpowered the negativity I saw around me.

Although, I had to be realistic, I started to find more aspects of myself that took me away from my "wounded" narrative into one of actually starting to feel joy in life. I started to become aware of the shifts and transformations that occur in the process of healing and I began to recognize that I am able to be seen in the world for who I am.

I drew comfort from knowing I am no longer desperate to fully live, because I *am* fully living. I also realized I am only a part of the common humanity, which to me is a fine mixture of suffering, which I accept, and joy. When I can be consistently honest with others and myself about what I desire, and what causes me to disconnect from others and life, then can I truly enter into my authentic spiritual self.

I did not own misery and the truth came out that I was a complex person, yet not original. Constant honest conversations with my friends in AA, as well as a significant amount of therapy, have helped me gain a sense of connectedness and humility.

I took long road trips with my AA buddies to other out-of-town AA meetings and hockey tournaments. We listened and shared and then listened and shared some more.

I heard once that, "A closed mouth never gets fed." How true this is. And the more I could hear my voice, the more confidence I felt in my own skin.

The highly spiritual people and giants around me loved me, and never judged me. They allowed me to cry and get angry, and even act my silly self at times. I'm not sure who said it, but I heard once that a barrier to mental health lies in a person's perception—self-delusion, really—that they are "terminally unique."

I've also learned in my studies of addiction and mental health that it is common for people to feel they are the only one suffering in their madness. This perhaps is why mental illness can be a silent, isolating existence.

By listening to others both in AA and outside of it, I saw that people suffered the same basic human problems that I was experiencing, and I thought I alone experienced.

They say in our Big Book of AA that an honest self-appraisal is insufficient. I think that's what I did for much of my life.

I knew I was doing the hard work of uncovering things about myself through therapy and regular attendance at AA meetings.

Yet, I needed to maintain sometime of a daily habit to still examine areas that came up that threatened my sobriety and mental health.

Today I feel it's important to have at least two or three essential spiritual advisors on hand and one of them is actually YouTube. I often explore various lectures and Ted Talks about science, the brain, religion, human nature, politics, creativity, and all this really does it open my mind to explore and learn more and more. I'm like a sponge.

With careful examination, information technology today is a powerful source for sharing experiences and ideas. However, we each have a responsibility to critically think about who, where, and what type of information we are consuming.

Thankfully, being hyper vigilant has enabled me to figure out others' motives quickly and lets me analyze information I am taking in. There are many sick people and belief systems out there.

By the winter of 2020, I had been living in Attawapiskat for a year, of which I was proud, mostly from a job and career perspective. I was asked to take part of a specific training for health workers called "Indigenous Tools for Living."

Honestly, I have been skeptical of the countless movements and workshops that are said to provide "the answer" to "holistic living" and they seem to range from yoga to meditation practice and everything in between. I see people who take a weekend workshop somewhere on, let's say trauma training, and they've had some insight and breakthrough and want to share with others, which is good. Yet we have to be careful, too, because delivering any type of therapy takes years of specific training.

I think some of the people who practice trauma care or deliver mental health programs, or even who work as social workers, are unfit and have ignored their own demons and they can do more harm than good. But having said that, I can now usually tell with my gut if a facilitator is experienced and well-trained. If I can see this value I will become involved in more skill development for my job and I may grow personally as well. I usually always do.

In one session of the Indigenous Tools for Living workshop participants created medicine pouches for ourselves in which we dug away at some deep-seated shame and raw emotions.

What I loved in particular about this training was that it seemed to allow participants to be guided by their own willingness to be involved. There was no pressure and the exercises were very free and almost innocent and playful. Which are starting to be characteristics I identify within myself.

When it was my turn to share about my shame experience, I became vulnerable and I noticed something I hadn't noticed before. My right hand and arm started shaking uncontrollably. Then I started to cry. It was almost a trauma response and it felt difficult at first, but then I moved into it.

A very gracious facilitator sat beside me and asked permission to place his hand on my shoulder, and I accepted. It was such a safe feeling. As I felt more of the rawness, let's call it pain, I shook more and I decide not to fight it. I was shaking and shaking to the point, let's say I was living out the Elvis Presley song, "All Shook Up." Then the facilitator guided me to take my medicine pouch to my nostrils and breathe the medicines in.

144

At first it was hard to come back to a more stable place because I felt I was losing it. But I kept breathing all those medicines: willow bark, bear root, dandelion, wild rose, tobacco, cedar, sage, sweet grass. And after about a minute of being guided through the smelling of the medicines, I felt my hands and arms stop shaking and I started to wipe my eyes. I took deep breaths and began to feel settled in my chair.

Once I was settled again I felt this was the connection I had needed all along. As I mentioned, it was simple. We all need to feel safe to be open and vulnerable. This was what I was hungry for, this was what I suffered from. And now as a man I can start to see there was safety in the world. I wonder how many men who have been traumatized—and other survivors of childhood sex abuse—simply need a place of safety to heal?

I know in our world it can be very challenging for us to seek and find a place of safety. There is no guarantee that we may ever find a place in our whole life. But I always encourage people to keep seeking.

Self-Compassion and Mindfulness

In the summer of 2017, I literally fought my way to becoming involved in a week-long Self-Compassion Mindfulness Teacher Training, to the point where I think I seriously annoyed the administrators of the program. But I made it.

I travelled quite a distance from Moosonee, Ontario—where I was living at the time—to up-state New York and landed at a beautiful Zen retreat centre named Chapin Mill, just outside Batavia New York.

When I initially arrived I was having severe panic and worry, as I knew I was about to dig away at my psyche. When I checked into my room the first thing I did was go online and find the nearest hospital in the event I fell apart too much. I was in shock for a bit and asked for some peace to be curious about this fear.

Then a thought came: you know, I have been given a gift here to examine and explore something, and although it's going to challenge me and be difficult, I can withstand this.

I think I had a nap and called my mother. I woke up and went to get dinner and meet some folks. The rest of the week had its challenges, but there was major growth for me spiritually.

When I think of humanity and my slow connection to it, I recall completing a walking meditation exercise facilitated by my amazing teachers Christopher Gerber and Kristen Neff. I felt so grateful to have worked hard to get to a place to do this work and be amongst other like-minded folks.

It was a beautiful day and we were all guided to walk around the grounds. Some small slopes leading down to a small creek overflowed with a variety of flowers and grass. I walked across a small bridge and stood underneath a willow tree.

I was secure and comforted in knowing I was being a human being. I knew my access to Nature was something I cultivated and wasn't concerned about what the physical world was unfolding for me.

Sunshine was drawn through the trees and edges of this meadow. It was my dream and all the visions I had experienced that led me to this place.

After focusing on the meditative practice, I looked up and noticed the other participants walking and meditating, all separate in their own experience. It was comforting to see how I can be, and was, connected to this humanity. Sure, we may have all been wounded, but we shared that aspect of this amazing life.

I knew I was glowing and I saw others glowing too. And I remember even witnessing others healing in their own way, like me. I often refer now to watching all the participants—maybe 20 or so—as being extensions of the landscape. I realized we are the garden of this life.

Following the exercise, I knew I had to get grounded again in some respect and we all had an amazing dinner.

Actually the food at this place was phenomenal. It was high quality nutrition to the point where my stomach was actually upset from time to time. But it was nourishing. Eating together was also a silent practice and I took this time to reflect and get firmly planted again. I will forever be grateful for the leaders who put this on and were able to have a spot for me to register.

To conclude in this understanding of my awakening with respect to humanity, I realized I had to work at establishing healthy solid connections that worked for me. God would not allow me to go through this life without experiencing the gifts of what others have to offer.

Today, I feel I have a healthy sense of connection and there is an ideal of intimacy I am trying to work towards. I fail many times in reaching my ideal, yet this is progress. I know I have a faith in others that is healthy for me, and that I can reach out if I need to. Some of my friends in AA and outside of it typically go through what we call an annual or semi-annual housecleaning. That works for me.

They might enroll in a spiritual retreat, meet new people, share. And generally just actively participate in an on-going discovery of the self, of connection, and of experience.

Just recently, I realized that if I go through this life knowing I was able to truly love at least one thing, I am satisfied. This one thing is turning out to be the adventure of my life

Awakening could be as simple as laughing at this and saying, "you know, it's okay you don't give a shit, why did I put so much expectation on this?"

Sharing Too Much

Another important awakening happened when I started to see that it was important for me to notice when I over-shared in social situations.

I knew sometimes I would feel awkward when I thought back to a time I had spoken up and I would feel a sense of shame around the fact that maybe I had shared too much personal information. The trick is to find ways to safely reflect on aspects of ourselves we have to change to survive.

I knew I was getting healthy when I started to call myself on my own shit. There came a point when I truly recognized I could not live alone with my insights into my consciousness, dreams, hopes, and faith, when I recognized I was falling into self-doubt and fear and disconnection.

Today, I am able to escape back into the fellowship of life and the goodness that comes with humanity.

One year, when I celebrated an Alcoholics Anonymous (AA) anniversary, I asked my home group of Early Bird to engrave, "Faith Without Works is Dead" on my anniversary medallion. This gave me a taste of freedom and my fears subsided. I was hungry for more and today I actually feel more fear when I am no longer hungry, because freedom and hunger go hand in hand for me.

Over time, I started to see that I needed to spend less time examining how my thoughts, behaviours, and negative decisions affected my morals. I became more at ease with life. I leapt into addiction-related programs, therapy groups, seminars, and retreats, any invitation, in fact, that would allow me to grow.

Sometimes—and this may happen for many people—when confronted with your own crisis, the real shock of a life event will enable us to have a brief moment of insight and clarity into the person we are. This is what I call a deflation of the delusional self.

Being aware of how we have behaved is frightening but very healthy. I struggled with memories of having been self–destructive, and of having harmed others out of fear.

I worship the times that I can have space to be open and feel safe at the same time. This is my religion, it's called Safety and it comes with the feeling that your soul is being engineered into something greater, and stronger.

The science of self-awareness is actually about witnessing yourself shift into different thinking behaviours, and responding to all of life accordingly. And for me it's also been about realizing that my questioning is a seeking of solutions and meaning, a sense of faith and a trust in a process.

The ultimate shifting again occurred through my deeds and daily actions to simply do well at every turn. To be expanding and remaining willing to actively engage in an exploration of myself and see my life experience as an adventure. To be willing to take in the truth about myself and acknowledge the importance of my relationship with my higher power, or God, or Creator.

Running through my recovery literature is a theme that supports the idea of being hungry for the opportunity to practice honesty. I accept that each day I may fall short of where I would like to be in life. However, I truly feel like I am mostly content.

]In my self-reflections I am increasingly aware of the natural lighthouse in my heart that has always been in place. I have been noticing each day that I am a part of an absolute transformation and it's amazing.

As I mentioned previously Awakenings have had a strong place in my life, through music and art. Even early romance was an awakening to life in a way, as were movies and their soundtracks.

I recall I formed a strong connection with the romance of boyhood in the movie *Stand By Me,* as it represented something I knew could yet exist for me, and it reminded me that I could still create memories of wonderful experiences. By identifying with these types of films, I saw the importance of movies in healing.

Real Change

What happens when we have a new thought, a new idea? It represents real change. And it results in action. I never thought it would be possible to change my rigid, selfish thinking but I learned through the principals of recovery, and my studies in psychology, to observe my behaviour.

No one in my social circles ever investigated the idea of self-centredness, or feelings of deep-seeded selfishness. Terms like "dishonesty" and "rage" and "lust" were never discussed.

This awareness of who I am and what I need and want is a new connection to a self that was foreign to me when I first began recovery, and once this connection started to form, I realized I was unstoppable. I started to really see that I was becoming healthy. For a long time, I stopped talking about how I was feeling and I asked for help. I had a desire to hear how I was doing in life and recovery, and this was a form of being kind to myself. It's said the ability to accept a compliment is a sign of being confident.

In the past, before I grew healthy, when I started to share how I was feeling, I felt I was almost delusional and maybe I also had a bit of social discomfort. I really believed that I was confident in what my feelings were, and what my thoughts on life were, yet this was another form of fear. I felt I had to maintain the balance of power in life's situations, I had to feel that I was in control and enmeshed in my own bullshit.

Now in true healthiness, I have developed a new confidence. I now value my beliefs and value my knowledge, yet I need to ensure that I continue to practice much humility and balance my knowledge with humility. I need to ensure Im respectful of my awakening experience and I've done this by expressing my honest desire to meet myself through any crisis with the willingness and courage to face what I see. Knowledge may not keep me alive, yet courage and faith will.

Living in faith has proven more beneficial to my awakening spiritual self than any knowledge has. In recovery lingo this is called "having intellectual self-sufficiency."

In addition, emotions and logic will only take you so far. Eventually everyone may have to face their own self-deception. A friend of mine said we can have a tendency to feed ourselves bullshit sandwiches and I can relate to that. My negative thoughts can be demons at times. These are brainchildren, and they can become distorted. Sadly, in the process my behaviour and thoughts can mimic patterns of despair, and many times I've resorted to living in suicidal ideation, suicide on the installment plan.

I believe feeling dead inside is actually the time we're most alive as we aren't distracted by false sensations of aliveness through substances, foods (in particular my craving for butter tarts) or behaviours (excessive shopping, love and sex addictions).

A major breakthrough for me in the past few years of my life occurred when I realized how many masks I wore, in every situation in life, in every interaction. I escaped by masking my core issues, like fear of intimacy, and personality problems.

It wasn't until I traveled up to James Bay region that I started to grow up in many ways and become more grounded to the human experience. I started to not live less in my head.

In my daily meditative practice now, I open and close my thoughts and emotions with comfort. I notice the silence and distance. I am aware of the connections within my life experience: clouds and darkness, obscurity, shared harmony, and pain with humanity. I appreciate that thoughts and life are impermanent and always changing, much like the tide and winds and gravity.

Distance within the vastness of the frozen landscapes here has naturally created a space to be open. I can see more clearly how my pain, sorrow, life and beauty are interconnected with the land and people. Living in the North, many healthy memories come up for me by simply standing in twilight, with strong winds and smells from my fire. I can meditate in freedom.

On a recent occasion, I walked along the Attawapiskat River shore and sensed a deep transformation in my brain. I could smell the dampness of grass beneath thick layers of ice, the smell of sweet grass and ice; I could smell the ice melting on the rocks.

Each step I walked I could feel the warmth of sunshine covering me, guiding me in silence. These were the miracles that began to flood my existence; noticing my breath and breathing is a major awareness. This was the soothing I remembered in my youth and the Universe that carried me through many nights of darkness.

151

The ice breaking up, and shooting towards the sky reminded me of scars, the many wounds the land carries for us. But also its healing and changing as we also walk with it.

In my eyes tears of goodness and peace rose up and I was again grateful for my place in this life. Although this gift of freedom was given to me, I knew in order for me to keep it I had to remember the work I needed to complete here in Attawapiskat.

Mystery and Uncertainty

I think in our current society we are so driven to have answers for everything we've forgotten the value of mystery and uncertainty.

Mystery cautions us to examine our experiences and the energy we invest in our lives seeking and wanting.

Mystery also teaches us humility. It teaches that we ought not to place people, places, and things above the health and love that mystery brings.

We are to be careful of sharing our life experiences with the world. Even sharing our danger.

I admit I at times get caught up in the energy of media and social life, however I am learning to recognize yet another important boundary I need to set related to how I seek assurance from life. Am I seeking comfort and security in the world, or assurance from the inner law within my soul?

Am I placing my value and ideas in believing and trusting that God is ultimately creativity to me, or am I chasing an elusive feeling of brief emotionalism and false connections with life?

Through spiritual examination I have understood more and more that in my life I need to cultivate consistency in my day-to-day life to have peace.

Fleeting false emotionalism with things and people do not cultivate a deeper sense of connection to a purpose for my life that I follow.

8   Short Essays and Poetry

A Summer's Poem

I recall the old path, growing with metal scrap, a small bronze lid from the ancient reservoir, the greens shadowing the clouds and the lights wave-hitting the bronze railroad. I sense rock, and wood soaked in oil, my bronze fearless chest hiking down the Battlefield Park in Stoney Creek Ontario.

The endless silver track piercing through the sumac, barely escaping a metal pipe beneath the old rock, my walk ending in laughter. Sitting on the concrete platform at the Rez.

Oh, how the dense, dark green vines covering the escarpment brought a pleasant sight to my eyes. The smells of limestone covered in fresh moss beneath the Devil's Punch Bowl in Stoney Creek. My home of blood and soul was stored in a different time and place in my memory.

The summer sun warming the grounds where I will walk in my youth and stand

My precious youth being and laying in the grass.

East Hamilton Delight

Heat on the train tracks, heat waves above the rails, the smell of the heat from the rocks and railway ties

Rivers remain, comforting his soul

Wounded shores are reformed

I am taking in a mad rush of cares from the Universe.

In the spring of 2018, I flew into the First Nation of Kashechewan to spend a week working as a child welfare professional.

As I walked up along the driveway on WaWe Yeston, I noticed an adult with a garbage bag in his hand and another bag full and lying stretched out on a mattress in the mud.

I looked down at the bag and saw a canine paw sticking out of it. Two young girls standing beside each other had their eyes glued on the bag, clearly experiencing sadness and confusion.

I asked if the dog had had a name. The adult, in a shaking voice, said, "Caesar." Caesar had been only about two years old, still a pup, half Husky, half mutt. It was unclear what had happened to him.

I kept monitoring the mood at the funeral scene. The adult began to place another garbage bag around the motionless canine.

Periodic gusts of wind came in and around, opening the bag, and the observers caught glimpses of Caesar's fur flying up. One could imagine the dead paws once pouncing and digging for scraps on the reserve. As I looked at the two young girls, who continued to stare at the bag, I felt something needed to be done in that moment, some closure, some acceptance.

I remembered reading once that our first experience with death usually occurs when we see an animal die, a family pet, a bird, an animal who met with tragedy crossing a road, even insects we thoughtlessly swat to their deaths, and then comes the death of a grandparent. In my case, I remember how sensitive I had been as a child to the death of each season, and, in particular, the autumn.

I took a deep breath and closed my eyes. When I opened them I looked around and on the ground a short distance away, I noticed a shiny Holiday ornament in another junk pile. It was a silver star. I reached down to grab it and then handed it to one of the girls and asked her to place the star on the bag and say goodbye. Although the girls still stared at the bag and what was left of their friend Caesar, the air had changed a little; there was a sense of calmness. I walked away and transitioned back to my day.

I can't avoid these moments, I jump into them, it happens so naturally to me, I see the details of life, of people's interaction with their lives, moments in which they're experiencing something profound. I gravitate to that and I'm given an opportunity to serve.

A Triple Grief

It has dawned on me that my emotions are under heavy grief brought through the loss of my marriage and friend of eight years—we had been together for 14—the loss of another brief friendship and, of course, the loss of my old self. This is all necessary for this part of my journey in life.

There is some validity in the idea that we have many losses, many experiences to grieve. I know that I have to stop searching for the old stones I threw into lakes and creeks and fields. Old stones bound to thoughts and memories I wanted to release. Perhaps we never really let go of these things.

Part of the sickness that I can create for myself begins when I start obsessing about continually going back in search of things I already released. I don't like that. At the same time, I also have moments of fleeting joy. I am comfortable in despair and sadness because it makes sense to me; for a long time, it protected me in some way. Making a conscious effort to go back to look at things that were already dealt with is a form of addiction in itself. I have identified many times that this is highly maladaptive.

The lost stones and old mistakes I made are there, but I choose to not shut the door on them, and, as a matter of fact, the Universe wants that door to stay open so I can still hear echoes of my experiences of love. I've been searching for identity all my life and the constant theme of my life has been to search and search and search. My interest in sociology has opened my mind about what I observe around me and I recognize that other people are searching for their identities everywhere, too. And searching for meaning, as well. We are often distracted. Why?

I have selected identities that I wanted the world to see—what I wanted others to think I was, or could be. I wanted to be somebody that I wanted the world to want me to be.

I did not have the skills to distance myself from this idea, or to form my own sense of identity and, to put it simply, I believe we live in a time when we are not truly empowered to be our own selves. We are often looked at as unordinary or silly or weird. Fuck that shit.

As the years passed, I kept wondering why I couldn't have the same peace of mind I had when I first got into Alcoholics Anonymous in 1996. And the answer is simply that I have evolved.

My peace comes from the action and quality of faith I can get out of myself more frequently. The healing is different because my faith is different.

When I first got into recovery, I met many loving people who didn't judge me. And this was where I was truly able to be myself. So, I began to write more. People today always say they remember I always had a note pad and pen with me because I wrote and sketched everything around me. I have had difficulty with simplicity most of my life. My thoughts are often random, and I have always complicated things for myself, made things more difficult than they need to be. Writing has always come easy to me. I recall a teacher in elementary school signing me up for a creative writing class in Grade 4.

When I dig deep into my madness I can see a new familiar language, one that is familiar to me. I struggled with feeling invisible growing up and I often felt I didn't have a voice, so I guess we can say that my writing has become my voice.

Listening to my heart draws me out of the madness, my clear physical self, and my undivided mind. But it's always the language of my soul, which speaks directly through my heart, that pierces through first.

Although there are many schools of thought now that recognize emotions and empathy to be harmful if we wallow in them or expect to navigate life purely on emotional intelligence. This may be due to the fact that too much empathy may prevent us from taking action.

Wounded Healer / Lee Lyttle

Old 27

So many places I've seen
On this highway.
Can't shake the shame
Can't shake the remorse.

They always tell me
I have a bit of Heaven in my heart
They tell me I got the cause

Who was lost, anyway?
We were closed off,
Lost in unchartered territory.

Maybe I'm obsessed with my emotions
That's why I like the sorrow a song can bring.
I am in almost constant repair
A constant patching of brokenness
A downed bridge in major reconstruction
Some days the repairs are minor,
A call for loss.

It's sad to me that I was searching for something I knew deep
inside I could not reach.

Yet I, too, was lost
And could not find you
But who am I to think I got it?

157

Wounded Healer / Lee Lyttle

Drop Attack

*I am being trained as the natural guard at the harbor where my
soul connects with my body.*

I cross over this threshold,

Which is madness,

In my own mind,

Searching for a place to bury my old bones

And watch my old ideas sink.

I see some skin still hanging onto my frame,

This frame of physical being.

My battered body hangs onto the wounds

From past wars

My skin of this world has protected me in some way

It carries my soul.

Now I am hungry for a new survival

New bones

New territory.

You say I have an old spirit, an old soul

Could this have frightened you?

But now my old spirit is dying

And a new soul is on the horizon.

Wounded Healer / Lee Lyttle

I Dream

I had a dream

I was on a stage and when the curtain came down. I peeked my head out and I said

"Don't be afraid of change."

The Universe demands that we change often to keep pace with it.

When the flares of the stars cross the horizon, there I witness myself, tagging along.

In the stars.

During my adventure in the skies I see old souls frightening those who are trapped.

In my flight, parts of my bones are born within a star that I follow

I recognize this star as having been travelling alongside my cosmic road already.

Veins

We enter this world like thunder,

Leave like thunder.

This doesn't make us special.

There are many incidences of thunder

We enter dreamland in frail, crackling temporary journeys

The light has reached me

A light that is growing deep.

Wounded Healer / Lee Lyttle

Skin

My Heart is more than vital flesh
My skin fights with the heart always
This is pain.

Each craves a relationship with the other.
My flesh needs to carry my heart and my heart desires connection with the flesh.
Yet how many times have I betrayed my own heart
And let my desires go?

When we are no longer blind to our egos,
Blind to our defects,
We can gain new insight to the reality of our moment
I suppose we fight a little for ourselves in daily storms,
And years of old ideas break out of our violent minds.

The pain that our distorted minds have kept break through a wall
When we are not feeling alive, so what is our solution?
Run, wait.
Awareness happens when we begin to see patterns of ideas and beliefs that are false.
It's when we embrace the uncertainty and the reality of who we are.
We embrace a little of the person that the world also sees

Going Down Old Roads

Understand this:

The ultimate consequence of the multiverse is

That you are loved.

Surrender

Darkness fell around him. His friends shouted, "You are a warrior." In that moment he faced life and took his river of life by storm.

All the hurts that he shared with the night and moon.

In my days I see my wonder.

I see my surrender.

Obscured

We drifted like clouds,

Protected for some time or place.

In some moments

We had colour.

Now It's Fired up in Me

The flame of my being is the beacon to return and light the fire inland

I stood on a new horizon:

Frequent waves of light stormed around me

And glimpses of a shameless soul within

have now become great moments in my day.

My bond is now with my soul and what a fantastic adventure it has become.

I see many horizons setting each day:

My soul sits on the hillside with me now,

Looking out into the sea

With its childlike eyes, adventure and simplicity, and wonder.

Fear and curiosity cannot exist together.

My shore is my skin, sometimes rough, but filled with grace.

I am that ship that once was lost at sea. For years there was no distant light:

I couldn't see that the bay never grew tired of trying to reach me.

It was the light of me that had burnt out.

Wounded Healer / Lee Lyttle

Broken in Love

He still lived with brokenness

Yet his soul was free;

He brought some loose sweet grass

And when he reached a path,

He set the grass alight

And said to the Universe: "You may take my brokenness and my sadness."

And as the fire burned to the edge of the grass,

The flames reached the muddy ground.

He heard the wind reaching through the forest.

Pockets of sunlight danced around;

Pieces of life and parts of his shattered self rose up and

Moments of despair and uncertainty flew up around the trees for the wind to swallow.

A Voice

I am sitting down and resting in the clouds that my head is in

And I ask

How does having my head in the clouds affect me?

We all have fragile minds that often observe destruction and aggression,

Wounded Healer / Lee Lyttle

Yet we also have empathetic minds that teach our hearts.

We are fragile.

When I fall apart, I am being built,

Molten, shedding skins.

I value that I am faithful

I am also faithful to my old dying self, finding ways to hang on.

I had to see that I was worthy of honouring my self.

My new sight, new vision for life takes form across the frozen river

It's clear and wide open.

Honouring the old skin.

This is my light,

My new skin,

New identity,

Light my skin and soul.

They are on fire

Bones are bruises,

Battles are born,

Yet I still walk this land,

Running back in to my home of the soul,

To a place I've known.

My soul is resting and charged,

While my carnal self is battling the lands and isolation inside

My struggle with the flight of my pride...

Egos rise up and are lifted away.

The Garden Robbery

1.

I am capable of love, yes
I would give my life to be one of you.
Give your life
Give your life to be one of them.
It is when the heart finds the morning
 New life within me is born
A new path is formed
I have died.
I am the one thing left
And my old life is dying away.
I see myself watching myself die away.
I saw myself get taken away.
I am allowing that through God and the silver 24-hour medallion
I received at the Harmony Group of Alcoholics Anonymous

2.

There I sat in my darkest hour
God beside me, holding me
And I said, "I am hurt."

165

3.

I saw us together in a fellowship, working together

Standing tall

In unity and undying love through suffering,

Experiences of faith and renewal.

I saw for the first time the blue skies, the trees and birds, and I was only 20 years of age.

Then I heard your laughter, laughing our way through tough roads.

The road of harmony and happy destiny

What a wonderful gift to have a friend like you.

Soul and Shoreline

The battles within me are running deep,

They are swift and quick.

Madness is running through my stomach and I sit and feel.

God says to me:

"Your idea of your love for me is off, way off.

You need to love me more."

I see a beautiful story coming out of this: a story of forgiveness and love.

Wounded Healer / Lee Lyttle

God's love is greater than anything.

In my meditations I create a new identity.

I related to my journey as I see the relationships in Nature to flowers, trees everything above ground.

In moments in meditation I can envision the underground festering

The underground screams for the light but darkness and light have a relationship,

Although they don't see each other. I can see how this represents the areas that lay deep within me that have yet to be uncovered.

Patterns of despair, obscured by the sun, yellow and broken like a storm. My heart was bursting, hot, central, orange, drowning. I saw my heart as something I could not reach. It was years away from me.

Then in a moment I envisioned massive white clouds smashing through me.

I saw the multiverse, working in my dreams; it makes me powerless. Understand this, What is the ultimate consequence of the multiverse? What? That I am loved. My Heart is more than vital flesh. My skin fights with the heart always, This is pain.

Each craves a relationship with the other. My flesh needs to carry my heart and the heart desires to connect with the flesh. Yet how many times have I betrayed my own heart? Let my desires go?

What does survival mean to us, anyway? We say we want to make the world a better place for those that follow. But do we really care? We won't know exactly what will be of the world when we leave. Survival is really a method when we are no longer blind to our egos,

Blind to our defects. I suppose we fight a little for ourselves and years of old ideas break out of our violent minds. The pain that our distorted minds have kept break through a wall.

When we are not feeling alive, what is our solution? Run.

Wounded Healer / Lee Lyttle

I was disturbed, shaken to my bones, I saw my duality, my painful self, and I felt the comfort and sacrifice of my other shadow self. This is when I was created. Born in pain and suffering. I felt comfortable sitting in the darkness, A darkness that leads to futility. A Darkness that can also lead to peace.

Dreams of Crying

As the storm grows

My blindness surrounds me

Yet a new vision is forming:

walking up to the field

the more lonely I was the more the sky and cliffs and oceans in my dreams cried out to me.

Behaving lost and full of fear, cornering me atop the fire escape then forcing me to climb down in to the belly of my eternity

Life was the study and I was the blood.

I have an old spirit, old soul. Could this have frightened you? But now my old spirit is dying, And a new soul is on the horizon.

Going down old roads, Hold on to me, Here's a turn.

Meeting you in the new Multiverse

We meet in new Territory under the skies.

On a path deep beneath the snowscape one winter in my youth I reached my soul on one occasion. It was again another memory of where the winter and white landscapes made everything around me clean and pure

Through intense terror and blows of despair, I recall sitting on a hillside, paralyzed. It seemed like I had spent years living in self-delusion.

The Universe shared with me time and friendship, above all else. They were years of hope and despair. Years of laughter and sadness. Yet, the Universe always stood silent in the distance.

There were many moments when Darkness fell around me and I went under, as if I were drowning in a river. I held within me all the hurts that I could. I shared them with the night and moon.

In my darkest hours, I saw only shadows. Many times they would frighten me, but now I see shadows differently. They help me see the opposites in everything, plus the way they move is cool. Especially when I see shadows from trees hitting the ground from moonlight.

On one occasion, a light from the sun came piercing through the window of the room in which I sat and hit the back wall in the room. Then the warmth hit my shoulder and I closed my eyes. I began to see that our journey, as they say, never really ends. The experience of the sun shining on me was real. It was the warmth I was seeking and something I needed that I may not have received fully before that moment. In many ways this is why I love the daily journey I take to find the light and shadows and warmth.

Recognizing when the Awakening is occurring has been the greatest awakening of all, simply because it teaches the hard lesson that I am not in control, and this is a relief. It is essential to my growth to know in every moment that I am not in control of anything.

Looking back, I see the positive consequences of surrender. Within my surrender I catch a glimpse of my actions from outside my body. The behaviours I am aware of cause me discomfort, like the act of seeking attention or lust. I am waving my hands. Yelling in panic, crying, fighting and, in the same moment, surrendering to the Cosmos and allowing myself to awaken in more connectedness to a higher power. My gut turns and my jaws clench, there is a shifting in my mind, a peeling of the wall around my heart. And I hear myself speaking and trembling: please take my grief, take the pain of losing my dreams.

I knew my soul was always hanging in the air around me, watching me unfold. A long moment of stillness comes over me and I hear my soul's comforting voice; I choose to sit with the pain and accept that its only purpose is to motivate me. Far better than my old perception—that it was out to destroy me. Change will always bring some discomfort, but not nearly as much pain as before when I caused unnecessary suffering by resisting myself. I hear that voice grow stronger: "You've changed," it says.

I Am Loved

In further contemplation I determine that I am loved in both the chaos and isolation of the Cosmos, and the mystery of the plan of a cosmos, and I am both. I can be hostile, restless and cruel, yet I am kind and compassionate, sacrificial, willing. I can act out in irritability and immaturity and show complete attention and compassion to others and myself.

As I slowly continued on a progressive healthy pattern of making connections with healthy people in recovery and outside of AA, and sorting out who was unhealthy for me, I was often confused about who I truly was, but this confusion came along side with an on-going effort to explore and discovery deeper aspects of myself. This confusion at times showed up as restlessness and anxiety, and vain attempts to connect with others through people-pleasing behaviour, and the pretense of caring.

Wounded Healer / Lee Lyttle

Through deeper connections with others in dialogue and sharing experience I was able to take home and examine how things applied to me. Through these examinations I grew more curious and found myself signing up for random workshops through university, college and my places of employment, everything from brain science, brain injury, cognition, psychology and creativity.

I signed up for day or weekend workshops regarding music, one in particular I loved was a Moog synthesizer series of workshops set up through the music store Long and McQuade. I suppose some friends and family thought I was obsessed with my desire to explore new things. In some respects, I also became aware that perhaps my need for constant involvement was a sort of spiritual bypass to still avoid deeper conflicts that persisted, yet I saw being actively involved in life as a sponge crucial to my well-being. I knew at some point I needed to also accept that there was an overall plan for me and then get out of the way while still enjoying learning new things.

It was almost as if I felt I missed out and was anxious to bring myself up to par with life. Trusting that my place in the Cosmos, although I believed had the right amount of chaos and stability, I had to continue to find ways to get grounded. I had to accept moments where I was the master and engineer of my own confusion and chaos. Luckily I had close friends who kicked me in the ass once in a while in this area of life.

All in all , with further contemplation, I was driven to really immerse myself in the actions of truly living life and becoming authentically involved in reality. It felt good that through actively living life I no longer had to live solely in my head. The math was simple really. The more "into action" I became, the more life became whole for me and fulfilling. I could see day by day an abundance of possible connections with others that were healthy for me. My perspectives changed after involving people in my experiences. As connections grew, I began to sense that my awakening was deepening and I started to see I wasn't just surviving any more but I was thriving. What an amazing gift and place to be after all the hard work I was doing.

My spiritual learning and lessons have frequently unfolded in this manner. Where there has been a major event or upheaval, I will go into a trance; my imagination begins to stir.

I am able to witness myself in complete disruption and I can sense that I am changing; my attitude and ideas begin to shift.

They say that God shows up through people in many ways, and I believe this. There are thousands of moments and experiences where I know certain people have been placed in my life to teach me something.

Holding Space

I am able now to find a space, and I have borrowed the term "holding space," to be vulnerable and it feels safe to examine my thoughts and emotions without intense fear, without being traumatized enough to run and avoid. This primarily is what happens in psychotherapy: new ideas help shift old ideas.

I grow more content each day. New awareness is being formed in simply recognizing my own defective patterns and examining their purpose.

Sometimes I fall into fear and run and avoid; I break when I find that I am consciously avoiding my inner struggle, I break. Then something stops me in my tracks. The beauty of recognizing and examining patterns is that it often connects me to change in a gentle way.

I recall how difficult it was for me growing up when I was being rejected in a social situation; I'd feel the added discomfort of self-pity, usually in tears and in private. I also felt I had to act out and be silly in social situations, or even pretend I was insane. I can see now this was just another way to deal with anxiety.

People I trusted challenged me to see conflicts going on within me that I could not see. I had to hear their words repeatedly.

Then it became my responsibility to realize I was holding on to old ideas of survival, old incomplete social skills that I thought were helping me thrive.

I had to distract myself from making important life decision, creating a to-do list of unnecessary items, which only contributed, to my feelings of being overwhelmed by life. Then I blamed life's demands instead of looking at how I created my own shit.

Now I laugh about all this. Releasing old ideas and patterns allowed me to see how many years of self–loathing and self–obsessing had caused me disorders.

To keep myself grounded in life I valued my connections with like-minded folks and often needed to cut off closed-minded folks. Having a sense of being grounded through good conversations is an ultimate tool for me that I cultivate.

Honest dialogue is just as important as air and food. These are conversations of survival. Having a safe place to share our deepest worries, or shames, is, to me, the greatest medicine for life and mental health.

I have to admit I still struggle with social situations and I think it's because I get into a state of hyper-vigilance related to wondering, "Is this a person I can trust?"

Many nights in my early recovery, I spent on the phone with other AA members and also visiting the home of my first sponsor, Bruce Carson. I felt like an orphan, but many nights he and his family had me over for dinner and I recall one evening we were having a roast and mashed potatoes and peas for dinner.

Bruce distracted me and I turned my head and when I looked back at my plate my peas were gone, vanished. I believe the family knew I had spent so much time cultivating seriousness in my head, to survive, that I needed to shift that. I can still fall into that trap today.

There were times when I had to work through the realization of how I was before. A weird panic that I had to deal with about accepting that my mind was broken in many ways. I once held a mind that wanted to turn in against me, yet it also craved peace.

I've begun to understand that my issues are primarily centred in my mind. This, I suppose, is the true ambivalence of my dual self, the relationship between my carnal mind and my soul.

I remember through my adolescence having intense moments of compassion, yet I would equally feel a sense of frustration about some major gap in my ability to build relationships.

I just couldn't build bridges for myself.

I now know I have an amazing gift for creating more opportunities to cultivate close relationships with family and friends.

I was, and am, so grateful I have a chance to experience something from this life that would otherwise be simply missing and out of reach.

I cross over this threshold, which is madness, in my own mind. Searching for a place to bury my old bones, and watch my old ideas sink. I see some skin is still hanging onto my frame, this frame of physical being, my battered body hangs onto the wounds from past wars.

My skin of this world has protected me in some way. It carries my soul. My shoulders and legs are my ship, my vessel. Now I am hungry for a new survival, new bones, and new territory

Many times I believed the work of healing required heavy reconstruction. It was important work but my growth always came through the reinvention of the old self. I needed to realize that it needed to die away. It was broken.

Poor Restless Child

Many damaged nights

I often wondered how I held onto remorse over not being compassionate enough.

But this was a demand far too heavy for me to carry

Wounded Healer / Lee Lyttle

I was eroding like soft soils in the valley.

She was within reach, then: distance.

My soul just rested by the valley and I knew

I in some way had to give permission for my soul to go into the valley.

When I sat, I could see my soul going into the valley, I was afraid of this separation. But then I remembered a story told of Mother Teresa, and how she had felt distant, and abandoned by her faith for long periods.

I detached, could see my soul now sitting by a river in a beautiful valley.

She is grieving.

The valley was more powerful than me.

In moments I hung on to where I could also take the soul out of me and see what it was saying to me;

I heard a voice say, "When you lose me, do not inherit a new form of soul.

I am it.

But you work."

A celestial rebirth begins

Elements of the Cosmos

Piercing through my lungs,

Clouds are rushing through me

Tossing me about a refinery fire, and reconstructing the authentic self of me.

Pain is the collapse that turns everything into beauty.

Conclusion

As I write now, I am yet again travelling and working in a remote part of Northern Ontario. I heard the other day that this place only touches the edge of the Arctic and it reminds me of the comment someone made about me: that I seem to be always living on the edge of the Universe.

I am drawn to places that are in transition, geography that is changing, people who are moving, structures that are falling and being rebuilt. Maybe this is because I have lived with a sense of instability and it helps me connect with the world.

I get overwhelmed when I think of how far I've come in my life. I have developed the capacity to move quickly into places I find safe. I have grown and become more disciplined— with the help of humility and the ability to be present as the multiverse shares more lessons with me. I always tell people we have to look at self-discovery as an adventure, enjoying the full circle of it all, because it may be experienced only once.

Over time I realized I was becoming more ambivalent, blind to my own character flaws. I would be struck by a morbid, crippling, defect, such as irrational fear, or self-pity—primarily in social situations—and it would give me a false sense of control.

Being willing to become more self-aware around some of my character flaws meant striving to experience a new type of comfort or security; seeing some flaws, minor or major, was better than believing I was deeply defective. Learning that one is self-delusional around certain realities is painful.

I often struggled with myself. Now, when I feel I am turning into a self–seeking person, I embrace it because I know it's a tool for further self-examination.

Again and again, as I built those bridges into my meadow, my resting place, I simultaneously felt a new comfort in my own resilience and in the courage I was showing in exploring myself.

I was a human being, living and suffering just like everyone else, yet I was content. Put simply: trauma may have been the ultimate wound that ill-prepared me for life.

I had known and accepted the fact that this life was going to be rigid. Now I felt I could face anything because I had access to a profound strength that was not my own.

I began to accept at this point in my life that the work God wants me to do in Steps 6 and 7 of Alcoholics Anonymous has begun:

Step 6—We were entirely ready to have God remove all these defects of character and

Step 7—Humbly asked Him to remove our shortcomings.

These steps have led me towards greater spiritual maturity. In my AA journey I knew I needed to walk through the threshold of this area in the 12 steps. Many in the program say that after stopping drinking we come to a point where we also grow sick and tired of living out unhealthy patterns in other areas of our lives as well, beyond alcohol consumption.

But the reality of Step 6 work was looking at how that old nature of wanting to run and avoid pain shows up in many other forms that are unhealthy for me and that have the potential to bring me back into deep despair and resentment.

Each individual at some point needs to cross this threshold if they want to truly overcome spiritual disease or, as they say, malady. This process teaches me more humility in life, which I need as much as sunshine and food.

I remember on one occasion In 2014 I was having a heavy bout of self-pity as though I had been thrown a hard ball with the major collapse of my marriage. While I continued to blame the world a friend simply said to me, "yes you tried, but you're not special—you're not the only one who has gone through this."

It's interesting that each time I fall prey to misery or anger, someone or something shows up to put me in place. Although my more severe character flaws may never fully be taken away, I have learned to correct my character through honesty.

I can see danger from a distance, but I will still walk close to the slaughtering of my integrity. A process for being aware of my flaws is a great gift but it comes at the cost of accepting my humanness; my imperfections are gifts because they hold me in the right place in the world, in humility and courage. And I can still walk towards greater connection with fellow humans.

With more awareness of subtle aspects of character that annoy me, I am learning I only need to be ready and willing to change for the better. It is quite a miracle that the wording in these steps—and most other spiritual or counseling readings I have—make so much sense to me.

Fading Away

At times, when I am in a period of heavy self–examination, I can still sense a part of me that wants to fade away and I say things like, "Fuck It." I get a real stinky attitude and, what's worse, I usually start forming negative thoughts and behaviours, self–loathing and self-pity. This idea has helped me accept that, although I will always have flaws, as long as I don't worship my flaws and allow them to consume me, and as long as I don't place them before my sobriety and my relationship with God, I can feel confident that I am on the right path to faith.

Flaws or character defects (or what some of my more religious friends call "sins") will in many ways always be a part of who I am. The question is, how can I work with them and use them for good?

For example, I know that some of my losses in life, in particular my marriage, were in many ways more difficult than quitting drinking. Yet I have been able to share many of my experiences with others who have been going through something similar.

Wounded Healer / Lee Lyttle

Through my story I may be able to provide some hope. It is a miracle that I can speak and provide hope to another person. When talking to newcomers to the AA group to which I belong, I see death fall away from their eyes and their crisis turns to hope. The individual who had been full of fears and confusion within a month will often show up 100% willing to engage in explorations that are sometimes painful.

Furthermore countless acts of humility helped me start to see my place in the Cosmos and I believe one process that a person—perhaps you, the reader—needs to experience is the deflation of the ego, the abandonment of the self. The process ultimately unfolds deeply, into your own vision of your place in the Cosmos. It may be difficult to do this with all the current distraction in our world, yet those distractions show us we need to be more diligent in our seeking for our own truth. Embrace it.

In discovering the process of a real spiritual connection, I believed my life was now a refining and recycling process of emotion and memory, the real experience of being driven to simply be a new person.

I found I needed to place this idea of a higher power in the centre of everything. Instead of defaulting to my old strategy, where I was in the centre of the Universe, I have learned to place the Universe in the centre of my thoughts and direction. For a long time I saw that my mind had been crafted by a dark past, and what I feel had been my soul's rough journey.

Sensing that my soul had been broken for a long time was a mysterious experience, and it remains so, today.

Now all I know is a time and moment in my existence. Now I no longer require myself to just accept things as if I think I know what is good for me, or even take responsibility for mending a damaged soul. I now engage in more active prayer and meditation than ever. Active, daily practice enables me to not feel I have to be in control of anything and it's the greatest freedom one could have. Through my entire trauma healing work and addiction and mental health recovery the main core belief was that I truly thought I would live for what I deserved.

179

For example, while working at countless temporary jobs after high school—everything from cleaning and wiping thousands of small bolts in crates at General Electric to working on an assembly line packaging English muffins at Oak Run farm bakery, I always said to myself, "I'm happy here and this is what my life will be." I just accepted it, but it wasn't truly for me. Maybe for others, but not for me.

With my new confidence in life unfolding more each day I was driven to create some success in my life. I was able to go back to college and university and study and feel confident enough to have an actual career in health sciences and counseling.

Never in my previous life did I picture myself walking across that university stage at Hamilton Place receiving a Diploma in Clinical Behavioural Sciences.

Nor did I dream I'd be a successful mental health professional living and working in a First Nations community at the centre of a state of emergency in Canada related to a suicide crisis for youth. But I have faith and believe these experiences in many ways are not of my own doing. I no longer have to take responsibility for parts of my soul that remain broken.

Being Responsible

In some ways I used to act out a victim narrative and now I can be responsible for all my behaviours and thoughts. It doesn't mean I will always try to be obedient and responsible, but I try.

I suppose we could say simply I was very immature and now I can embrace integrity in how I conduct myself.

A friend of mine told me recently that they recall seeing me in a very low state and that when I spoke it was confusing and as if I were in outer space. They then mentioned to me that, I now have weight to my words and there is meaning and purpose when I speak. This is the work of that mysterious creative life force.

The only effort I believe is asked of me is that I remain obedient to the process of what my soul needs to work out. To embrace the new person I am becoming and embrace the relationship to this old soul within me. And understand that I am driven to be in a constant state of awakening.

This process does not need to be linear and perfect, nor must it meet my expectations. Yet I am required to be obedient to any laws my soul presents to me in each moment of my breath. I am required to be present when I sense something is awakening within me, whether it is difficult or pleasant. I am required to recognize when freedom is occurring and, most importantly, to share this experience with others.

I have tapped into a well of self-compassion and the work was very difficult. But with a little hard labour, a little digging, and the act of allowing a force to dig deep into my heart, I am living with a person I never knew existed.

As I am developing as a Man, I begin to see and experience loss and it has been refreshing for me to realize, with the support of others, that I was able to feel lost in reality.

Flying in the North

My sessions in therapy within the past year have been fruitful and many breakthroughs continue to occur.

One of elements I try to be aware in my own practice as a professional is acknowledging what our bodies are telling us, and this is particularly valuable for those who have experienced trauma.

In a recent session with my own therapist I shared that after almost two years of periodically flying in to a remote community with an indigenous population I have noticed how my body and psychology have responded or reacted to this transition, this experience.

I talked about how about 15 or 16 minutes into my 20-minute flight from Moosonee to Kashechewan, I have been starting to feel a weight in my shoulders and neck which, as I get closer to descent turns into a heavy fatigue. I've noticed I get extremely tired when I land, and I feel as though I could sleep. I also feel in my body my forearms filling up with a sort of numbing sensation. I typically put my hands together and try to think of ways to release this energy. My therapist and I discussed why this might be happening.

I always try to use percentages in my own therapy practice so it's interesting that this method was used here for me. And of course this is just a number, but it's helpful. We determined that 75% of what I am holding is a mixture of my own anxieties about job performance: tasks I need to complete, normal work-related demands and also the stress and transition from travel and having to live away from home.

Work/life balance is another issue, as well as thinking about food—which is expensive and sometimes hard to find in the North. Then there is my passion for social justice and recognizing I am both a child welfare worker with mandated responsibilities and a crisis worker sometimes facing more issues that are seemingly outside the scope of mandated duties. This is my responsibility. I have found it takes me about a day to unwind and start to focus after these flights.

My therapist and I determined that 25% of my reaction to flying in to the North was perhaps the energy from the other travellers on the plane. I may be picking up on their stresses or whatever experiences they may have been having. These are not my responsibilities.

I suppose I was trying to reach a conclusion that there was much of me going on, yet there was a whole other experience in my working and living life in the north .We talked about the possibility of percentage in the community as being a mixed, sometimes chaotic, broken down system, with a fragmented community that has multiple, complex, social, economic, and spiritual needs. Some are being fulfilled; some are not.

Wounded Healer / Lee Lyttle

I reflected on how it's challenging for me because our child welfare-mandated system is so closely interwoven with these complexities and I have had to work hard to navigate it, sometimes with support and sometimes without.

Learning how to see how I am developing personally and professionally simultaneously is the greatest gift of being a professional child welfare worker/family therapist/social service worker/clinical behavioural science counselor. Hence I now self-identify as a "wounded healer."

Now I will say this: I am not identifying myself as a healer of anybody or anything with the belief and intention that this is a profound ability or gift that I have been given to bring to the world. Yet rather that my experiences in life combined with the knowledge and skills I've learned and practiced have afforded me great opportunities to contribute to this world. All in my desire to fight social injustice. I have had to learn what is within my scope and ability and where my limits are.

So, we talked about what the next step would be, where do I take this heaviness? Fortunately my therapist has seen visualization, meditation, and spirituality or faith as one of my strengths.

My therapist asked about my dragonfly tattoo. I explained my friend Rob V, owner of Grey Harbor Tattoo, had created it. I explained that it essentially represents to me my interest in the subconscious and also my interest in change, metamorphosis, transition, alternate realities and so on.

I had always been totally against tattoos as I saw everybody was getting one and I wanted to be different. But I liked the idea of what the dragonfly represents. I explained that this creature lives in two worlds. It starts underwater as a nymph and then climbs up a blade of grass or weed or twig to the surface of the water and enters the air and sky and land. I can resonate with this transition and, for lack of better words, metamorphosis.

My therapist was able to see this as a symbol I can again use as I am descending to land in an airplane, and visualize the dragonfly as a helper in my transition, helping me let go of the heaviness I feel. When the dragonfly is going through its transformation it is travelling from the underwater world as a nymph and into the air and earth. Also, once in the new world it doesn't return. This is the lesson I have encapsulated on my forearm in the form of a tatoo.

I am learning to breathe and visualize.

I can visualize the tension that may be festering in 25% of the passengers on the plane flow off the wings outside the plane. I notice that my perspective of aspects of the community is becoming more resilient and I notice that a unique sense of humour still flourishes—not only in perspective but also in reality. Aside from the negative images and prejudices that we see reflected in the media about Canada's indigenous communities, I have found in them a powerful sense of humanity.

My therapist and I talked about how I've had to learn I am powerless over what assistance I, as a human, can provide. This discussion led me to further reflect on my burgeoning sensitivity to everything around me. I feared these new intense feelings of sensitivity until others around me suggested it may represent a deeper level of spiritual awakening. I could relate to that.

I began to see how throughout my life I've been continuously transitioning from one environment to the next and now I can see that this process has been creative for me. Seeing myself as a human being, while understanding that I am learning to be human, has brought great relief. As my friend Brad says, it's absurd to see people walking around looking as though they believe they have been here before, that they know how to live life…when really, they're just as new to the world as I am.

Again, there is a great relief in accepting that there are no guarantees in life, and there is relief in knowing that I am powerless, that I actually don't have to be in control. And when I bring myself into the valley of despair within me, I will be strong enough to face my greatest enemy, myself.

The Great Refining

I have an image of my blood flowing within me and when I'm experiencing difficult emotions it grows thick and heavy.

Perhaps, it's a reminder of my physical self. It seems that it's all I have that is really breathing in me. I can see my mind growing closer to an emotional self I abandoned or never developed.

I have walked paths of terror, into my darkness, and I always ask, "Why do I keep going into the valley of despair of my own accord?"

Part of this sickness is that I want to feel despair and I become obsessed with feeling darkness; but I have the choice and power to exercise self-control. When I started to see an inevitable consequence that was healthy for me while in my despair I realized it could be a tool for seeking out new freedom and light.

Now my goal remains to share my human/spiritual experience while exercising my creativity, all in the spirit of playfulness and the nurturing of my imagination, while creating safe spaces for me. I aim to do this daily, so I can reach deeper meaning, and self-awakening. I encourage you to create safe places for yourself, to let yourself out and not be afraid.

Find and express your story at all costs.

Let your creative voice out.

The bandwidth for this edge I've always carried has only begun to fire up and now it contains more elements of mystery than I could ever imagine. The task of grounding my mind and my emotional self was no undertaking of my own, but rather flew from the energy of the celestial boundaries that have been constantly fine-tuning me, removing loose wires that still had white sparks, blue sparks, burning endlessly out of my elbows and shoulders. I believe a new transformation is always occurring within all of our experiences. Reading this book now, hearing my words, you are contributing to your own transformation.

Visiting Half Kash

In the late summer of 2018 I went for a drive after work to a little place called "Half Kash." It was a place that had always kept me grounded and I was honoured to participate in ceremony there.

I had been working for 19 months in the child welfare system at the time, grateful for my new challenges, digging deep into my need to serve for a cause and simply give back what had been given to me.

I had a vision of the accumulation of all my meditation experiences in one brief moment: *I saw the Albany River flowing by, chaotic in every direction. It was as though the sun's rays were guiding the currents in a dance with light and wind and force, and it saw its rhythm and method. I was again at another edge.*

I felt a heavy celestial—yet almost mineral—connection between my chest and the floor of the river, although I did not see it. I envisioned my breathing becoming chaotic and almost panicking, because I knew something major was about to occur.

The bandwidth grew larger. I could not harness myself and I fell at the top of the short riverside cliff. Pebbles and brown and grey clay from the shores lifted up in tiny pieces to break my fall. I was a star that was rising from the bed. My naked body floated for some time along the shore and the wind carried me up and over the river and back again. F

or some moments my body floated above the trees and I looked below at the ridges and edges of the bay. I saw other souls emitting blue and pink and yellow shades of light from their shoulders. My blood was shades of brown, like the river.

I saw voices pushing the molecules aside and I saw crying. The connections between the people to both the ground and the celestial elements were a force beyond comprehension.

I was satisfied by my own crying, satisfied with my skin and bones. I was happy for my own wounds for my wounds had come full circle. I was satisfied that my heart was where it needed to be. Beating in my chest.I was satisfied that I wanted to breathe.

Wounded Healer / Lee Lyttle

I am grateful every day and thankful for my life and I know this freedom in my daily visions represents the freedom I have from the gift of willingness to dig deep always, leaving no stone unturned, leaving no dark shadow unexplored.

There is always a sense of comfort in knowing I am involved in the shaping of this great structure in my life. The structure of accepting powerlessness and silence, the structure of a contemplative life, the structure of discipline and obedience to spiritual laws and the structure of mystery and grace.

Finally, through obedience and discipline I embrace Nature and the creative force and the human race that have a holding place where I can easily interpret what my soul is communicating to me. I seek to interpret in my daily practice a contemplative life, being both satisfied with what unfolds and sitting with mystery.

People ask me, "Why did you come to Moosonee, Ontario? Why are you doing the work you are doing?" I say my heart has a mission and has driven me here. Furthermore, I have been drawn in particular to the devastating event of a young First Nations girl who committed suicide at age 12. Many have said she was bullied at school. I find myself going frequently to her memorial site. I've never met the girl or her family, yet I feel there is a deep connection. In my spiritual life I have heard many people say that once you feel you are driven to a cause, you can't turn back. I have lived a life of being bullied and I have survived. This is my gift. My work, although a small fraction of what I really owe to God, is where I try to give back what was given to me.

Sharing Stories

It's taken me here. I want to share my story with males and other survivors of childhood trauma; I want others to know they have a voice. I have a particular drive for social justice, in particular with indigenous populations, as I know that some aspects of their sacred teachings and ceremonies have helped me to get where I am now.

187

In addition, my story of addictions and bullying is one I need to share so others know they, too, have this voice to begin their own healing path.

I also know I have had to be sensitive about this experience as I highly respect and value traditional teachings. I feel very fortunate to have been invited to aboriginal circles and I don't take these experiences lightly. I feel a great responsibility, spiritually and morally, that resonates deeply within me because, simply put, this life is very connected with the natural world.

I see trauma and I know how men feel ashamed of themselves. But now is the time to walk in no shame, walk in beauty, and the beauty of a man. The beauty of a human

One of the greatest gifts in my life is the opportunity to feel continual willingness to be aware of my own experience.

My hope is that you, the reader, will find your own inspiration and that you may grow in awareness of your own experiences and begin to heal. The healing of pain, grief, and sorrow grow in the awareness of being a full human, which also includes joy and abundance. Allow that to flourish in your imagination and daily actions.

My hope is that the reader may identify and avoid comparison, and see a process for unearthing your authentic self.

Old memories that are difficult, triggers in life, aspects of myself that I don't like…they will always continue to arise for me, and they may for you as well. I have learned to see that all these and more are opportunities for me to grow into a deeper spirituality and dig deeper into self–discovery, rather than a crisis of identity or a crisis of faith.

I often find that my feelings of being secure as a person and my feelings of joy and peace and serenity can also make me feel insecure simply because in this cruel world people sometimes will still judge a person for being secure. It's almost as though there is no real way for the world to just accept when people are hurt or they are happy.

Moving forward, I don't believe the world will ever change in many respects. This is also a test of humility again. I am okay with this because I love who I am. I am no one special.

Although I may have been able to have this gift and opportunity of telling my story, there are many more stories and experiences for others to share.

There is a growing calling in my heart that is digging more deeply into this life, and I feel like I can't control this love, I can't contain it. Nor do I want to contain it.

My voice is stronger than ever.

My mind is deep within my heart and is no longer a separate sense. My heart has a consciousness now that I've never known. It's a force that I will not try to explain.

There is a new light in my consciousness and a fire still burning more intense in my entire being that nothing will extinguish.

There is a quietness in my being unlike anything I have every felt. This quietness I felt holding me as I walked around the Dyke path in the little community of Kashechewan.

They say the meaning of the name of the river I'm walking alongside is "Fast Flowing Waters" and yet it's only running simultaneously with my beating heart.

I have so much inspiration where I live now, still searching for meaning and understanding at the edge.

It is in the moments when I find I am approaching a new edge in my existence that I see how my soul is constantly communicating peacefully with me.

I am wounded and I am healing through my simple voice and story.

Wounded Healer / Lee Lyttle

Awake

Once I was awake

Warm blue shadows from the wild land I sit in

Out of the river of deep blue

Each shadow and sparkle rising up from

Diving in and away from the ripples

Bringing with it

Winds of a new tomorrow

New blankets of white

In a new day

Shadows in our life striving

Do not be frightened when you witness your lights wrestling with the cold

Bring the warmth of a love you have fit yourself to.

Do not be frightened when you are going under and the current is fast

You will surface

You will cry for justice within you

Your Heart will flow on a new breath

Find the rhythm of the tide

Embrace the ever-changing wind and tide

We cannot be there long

But embrace that the springs and force are part of your veins

Remember we are the living

New Trails in the Woods

One day recently I was walking along the shoreline and found some new trails in the woods, there were some new season snow and some small ice formations in the grass.

My friend and companion in the form of fur, Lily P, a pure breed semi-haired Dacshund, was behind me following my every step. On the path I saw some fox prints and I stopped and pointed them out to Lily. She had a sniff and then kept exploring.

Today, I have a sense each day that I have been for many years already living in knowledge of having peace and joy and all the things that life is asking of me. And equally I have seen myself living through actions where I can feel safe and free.

That warm feeling of seeing snow and ice came over me again and I can see that meaning of the Dragonfly. My human experience is changing in front of me, from sensing my skin and body to trying to embrace and work through some chilly winds.

I loved the wind on my face and knowing I would find warmth again. That experience of arriving at a warm shelter to rest. I am blessed with experiencing seasonal changes because every time it helps me recognize the seasons within me.

It teaches me how I need to stay hungry for warmth.

For some time in the past three years since I started to feel this deep need to travel in the north, I couldn't understand what was happening to me. Certainly I was seeking a career change and maybe I was running a little again, rationalizing, maybe experiencing some denial about the pain I was dealing with from the loss of my marriage.

However, I knew I was also going to have to confront yet more deeper aspects of myself and I did not want to do that. There was no cure for me in the north, but finally one day when writing and having a fire in the woods, something hit me.

Amidst the white landscapes and ice and barrenness I see around me — and that I always come back to — is the belief that it's possible my trauma in childhood happened in the winter. I keep thinking my brain had an imprint of the landscape and season as sort of a time, space, and life that I once knew before my brain and my being were traumatized.

I believe God has placed me exactly where He knew I would need to do more work. It has been through this work that I found myself even more like a child and needing more obedience, yet I have been able to have the amazing freedom of innocence that I thought was lost forever. Through the silence of this land I have found that Grace has been staring right into my face.

So this is my solace. Silence, humility, spiritual and moral responsibility, gratitude and service. My heart can finally be resting in the space of God's grace, in knowing and being.

Resources

Suicide Crisis Support
https://www.crisisservicescanada.ca/en/
Call 1-833-456-4566
Text: 45645

Alcohol and substance use support
https://www.connexontario.ca/links
1-866-531-2600

Male Survivors of childhood sexual abuse supports
https://www.attorneygeneral.jus.gov.on.ca/english/ovss/male
_support_services/
1-866-887-0015

*God, grant me the serenity
to accept the things I cannot change,
courage to change the things I can,
and wisdom to know the difference.*
- Reinhold Niebuhr

Manor House Publishing Inc.

www.manor-house-publishing.com.

905-648-4797